"Of all the branches of men in the forces there is none which shows more devotion and faces grimmer perils than the submariners."

—Winston Churchill
British Prime Minister

Sweet Carolina
MYSTERIES

Roots and Wings
Picture-Perfect Mystery
Angels Watching Over Me
A Change of Art
Conscious Decisions
Surrounded by Mercy
Broken Bonds
Mercy's Healing
To Heal a Heart
A Cross to Bear
Merciful Secrecy
Sunken Hopes

Sweet Carolina
MYSTERIES

SUNKEN HOPES

Gabrielle Meyer

Guideposts

Sweet Carolina Mysteries is a trademark of Guideposts.

Published by Guideposts Books & Inspirational Media
100 Reserve Road, Suite E200
Danbury, CT 06810
Guideposts.org

Cover and interior design by Müllerhaus
Cover illustration by Bob Kayganich at Illustration Online LLC.
Typeset by Aptara, Inc.

This book was previously published under the title *Sunken Hopes* as part of the *Miracles & Mysteries of Mercy Hospital* series.

ISBN 978-1-959634-69-0 (hardcover)
ISBN 978-1-959634-81-2 (epub)
ISBN 978-1-959634-80-5 (epdf)

Printed and bound in the United States of America
10 9 8 7 6 5 4 3 2 1

SUNKEN HOPES

Chapter One

Evelyn Perry studied the museum blueprints, trying to appear busy, but her attention wasn't on the piece of paper in her hands or even the carpenters working around her. All she could think about was the appointment she had scheduled in ten minutes.

The sound of hammers, power drills, and conversation filled the large room in the Angel Wing of Mercy Hospital. Skilled workers constructed display cases, complete with solid maple bases and plexiglass lids. Soon, those cases would be filled with the artifacts that Evelyn and her team of curators had painstakingly selected for the past several months. Items that would tell the complex and unique history of the famous Charleston hospital.

"Evelyn!" Anne Mabry entered the new museum, her eyes wide with curiosity and excitement. She was a dedicated volunteer at Mercy Hospital and a good friend. She was just as enthusiastic about the museum as Evelyn. "This room looks amazing. I can't believe the transformation."

Evelyn smiled at her friend as she set aside the blueprints, eager to give Anne a personal tour. "What do you think of the color we selected for the walls and carpet? Too bland?"

Anne's gaze slid over the room. Evelyn had chosen a charcoal-colored carpet, made for heavy foot traffic, and paired it with creamy gray on the walls. Large, plate glass windows looked out at the Grove, a beautiful green space along the side of the hospital. They were still in the midst of the installation phase, but Evelyn had been assured that the carpenters would be finished today. They were putting last-minute touches on the exhibit panels, display cases, and lighting. All the room needed now were the actual artifacts that would tell the story.

"I think it's perfect," Anne said, slipping her shoulder-length blond hair behind one ear. "I still can't believe this is becoming a reality. After all this time."

Evelyn inhaled a deep breath, reveling in the sights and smells of the remodeled space. She had dreamed of adding a museum to the hospital for years, but the hoops she needed to jump through had taken longer than expected. Finally, six months ago, they'd been given the green light from the hospital board after Evelyn received a substantial grant to see the project completed. It hadn't been easy, since she was still expected to work her regular job as the supervisor of the records department, but she made it happen.

The door to the museum opened again, and this time Joy Atkins and Shirley Bashore entered. Their expressions matched Anne's, making Evelyn feel proud of the work they had accomplished in such a short time.

Joy was the manager of the hospital gift shop, and Shirley was a float nurse who worked wherever her expertise was needed. Both of them were relatively new to Mercy but had quickly become friends with Evelyn and Anne.

"This looks wonderful," Joy said to Evelyn. "And to think, this used to be an old storage room at one time."

"A storage space, hospital rooms, an old entrance," Evelyn amended. "There's almost no telling all the ways this space was used for the past two hundred years." The Angel Wing of Mercy Hospital had a fascinating history. Built in 1829, with beautiful red brick and charming gables, the building had stood the test of time. It was nestled in the midst of the historic district in Charleston Harbor and served as the general hospital for the local citizens, though it was also a popular tourist destination because of its history. When a fire tore through Charleston during the Civil War, everyone thought the structure was lost. But after the ashes settled and the rubble was cleared, the citizens discovered that the Angel Wing, with its beautiful Angel of Mercy statue, had been spared.

The facility had been rebuilt and modernized over the past two centuries, but the statue and the historic wing were preserved. Daily, tourists drove by, trying to get a peek. Rumors abounded about hidden tunnels, secret passageways, and unexplained miracles.

What better place to put the museum?

It didn't hurt that it was right across the hall from the records department, giving Evelyn easy access.

"We know you're busy," Shirley said to Evelyn, "but do you have time to give us a little tour during our lunch break?"

Evelyn glanced at her watch. "I have an important meeting in a few minutes, but I can show you around until Cyril Lorenzo arrives."

"We don't want to keep you," Joy said.

"The meeting will be here," Evelyn explained. "And you might like to attend, if you have the time."

"Sounds intriguing." Anne lifted her eyebrows as she glanced at each of her friends and then back to Evelyn. "Who's Cyril Lorenzo?"

Evelyn could barely contain her excitement, feeling like a child about to open a much-anticipated birthday or Christmas present. "The director of the Warren Lasch Conservation Center."

"Isn't that where they have the Civil War submarine?" Shirley asked, squinting her dark brown eyes. "I took Mama there this past summer. It was fascinating."

"You're right," Evelyn said. "The submarine is the *H.L. Hunley*. The conservation center has a special artifact they're loaning to us for the grand opening. We'll keep it through the summer, cross-promoting the two museums."

"That's exciting." Joy's face lit up with interest. "Is the governor still coming to the grand opening?"

Evelyn's pulse ticked a little higher at the reminder. "He is, which is all the more reason I'm anxious to get all the artifacts in place." She led her friends away from the door and into the heart of the exhibit floor. The natural lighting from the tall, tinted windows, combined with the museum track lighting, gave the room a warm, comfortable feel. A team of museum specialists from the South Carolina Historical Society had been working closely with Evelyn and were currently helping the carpenters with display cases. The plan was to start installing the artifacts tomorrow, though it would take over two weeks to complete. Evelyn hoped to have a few days on the other side of the installation to do a final cleaning before the grand opening.

The exhibit panels, with information about the history of the hospital and how it had impacted Charleston, were already installed. They were impressive, made of top-quality materials.

"I couldn't have done any of this without the South Carolina Historical Society," Evelyn said to her friends. "They've been wonderful to work with and so professional."

"It's easy to see they know what they're doing." Shirley stopped to admire a panel that showed the history of the Angel of Mercy. A life-sized picture of the statue was set against a beautiful blue sky. "This is such a great addition to the hospital. Well done, Evelyn."

Evelyn's cheeks warmed. "It's a team effort, to be sure."

"But it was born from your vision." Anne squeezed Evelyn's arm affectionately.

The main door opened, and Evelyn glanced up to see Cyril Lorenzo enter with a small metal case in his hand.

"He's here," Evelyn said, her voice betraying her excitement.

The others looked in the same direction but stayed back as Evelyn went to greet her special visitor.

"Hello, Mr. Lorenzo."

"It's nice to see you again, Mrs. Perry. I've brought the coin."

The lead curator from the South Carolina Historical Society, Adam Chilton, joined Evelyn and shook Mr. Lorenzo's hand. Adam was a thirtysomething with a shock of dark hair and black-rimmed glasses. He had been excited to help Evelyn from the beginning and was instrumental in working out the loan from the conservation center when he learned the connection between the twenty-dollar gold coin they possessed and the reconstruction of Mercy Hospital after the fire.

"Where would you like it?" Mr. Lorenzo asked him.

"Over here," Adam said, indicating that everyone should follow him. He led them to a corner of the museum, sectioned off with plastic hanging from the ceiling. There, he was housing some of the other artifacts that had already been returned to the hospital. Over the years, Mercy had loaned out their artifacts to neighboring museums and historic sites. With Adam's help, Evelyn had started to recall the loans. For the most part, the other organizations were happy to hear about the hospital museum and had gladly returned the items. But there were still some who were sore about the recalls.

Evelyn wasn't worried about those today. Instead, she gave her full attention to Mr. Lorenzo and the gold coin he was about to reveal to them.

Adam cleared off one of the tables where he'd been documenting artifacts and indicated that Mr. Lorenzo could set the case down.

Evelyn stood nearby, while Anne, Joy, and Shirley stayed near the plastic wall, out of the way.

"You've taken all the proper precautions with security?" Mr. Lorenzo asked Adam and Evelyn, his gaze serious.

"We have," Evelyn assured him. "All the locks are in place, as well as security cameras on all the exits to this room. No one will touch the items unless they are preapproved members of the team. Adam and I will personally oversee anyone who handles the coin."

Mr. Lorenzo nodded and then had Evelyn sign several forms before he was ready to open the case.

Everyone looked on eagerly as he unlatched the box and lifted the lid.

Nestled in a bed of black velvet was a Civil War–era twenty-dollar gold coin, indented from a bullet and inscribed on the back. It said: *April 6, 1862, My Life Preserver.*

"Why is the coin so special?" Joy asked in a hushed tone.

Mr. Lorenzo stepped aside so the women could get a better look and said, "It was given to Lieutenant George E. Dixon by his sweetheart, Queenie Bennett, before he left to fight in the war. She gave it to him in case he needed supplies, but he kept it in his pocket as a way to remember her."

"That's sweet," Anne said.

Mr. Lorenzo continued. "Family legend says that during the Battle of Shiloh he was shot, but the bullet hit the coin, thereby sparing his life. In 1864, Dixon became the captain of the *H.L. Hunley,* the first successful submarine used in warfare, right here in the Charleston Harbor. Unfortunately, after the sub fired a torpedo and took down a Union ship, it never resurfaced, and the story of the coin became a legend."

"That *is* unfortunate," Joy agreed. "I've heard of the vessel but haven't had a chance to learn more."

"For over a century," Evelyn said, "no one knew what happened to it the night it went on its last mission. I think it was 1995 when they finally discovered it about a hundred yards away from where the Union ship was torpedoed, in only twenty-seven feet of water. Several feet of silt buried it and protected it from damage. About twenty years ago, they lifted it from the harbor and started preserving it at the conservation center. The archaeologists discovered the damaged coin with Lieutenant Dixon's remains, proving the family legend was true."

"And how does this coin connect to Mercy Hospital?" Shirley asked Evelyn.

"The Dixon family donated a great sum of money to help rebuild the hospital after the fire, in remembrance of Lieutenant Dixon. They were benefactors for many years, though we lost touch with them in the early twentieth century." She smiled with excitement. "I've been in contact with one of the Dixon family members, though, and she's coming tomorrow to see the exhibit."

They continued to admire the coin for several minutes, and then the women dispersed back to their jobs within the hospital, leaving Evelyn alone with Adam and Mr. Lorenzo.

Before Cyril left, he gave Evelyn a long glance. "I am entrusting this to your care, Mrs. Perry."

"Yes, I know." She smiled. "I will guard it with all precaution."

"See that you do." He nodded once and then left the museum.

Despite Evelyn's assurance, she suddenly felt the weight of her responsibility.

The coin was irreplaceable. What if something happened to it?

It was already past six, and Evelyn was late. Mondays were usually her busiest days of the week at work, but with the addition of the museum, she wasn't sure if she was coming or going.

She pushed open the front door of her home, sagging in relief when she smelled the Italian aroma of the meal she had put into the slow cooker before leaving for work. At least one less thing she needed to accomplish before her brother and niece arrived.

"Evelyn?" James called from the kitchen. "Is that you?"

"It's me." She closed the front door and put her keys in the antique calling card dish on her hall table. The narrow two-story home she and James shared was painted a cheerful, creamy yellow with lots of white trim and Charleston Green shutters. The famous color graced almost every Charleston Single House on the historic street she and James had called home for the past thirty-four years. Evelyn's house, like the others, was only one room wide, and originally boasted a two-story piazza on the side, which had been enclosed by her parents when they bought the home in the early 1960s. The piazza was now a long hallway, running the length of the house.

"Did you pick up the bread?" James asked as he came out of the kitchen to greet her in the entry hall. He was wearing his usual polo shirt and slacks, having come from the College of Charleston, where he was the dean of history. He held a stack of plates with glasses balanced on top.

Evelyn showed him the bag of groceries, which was another reason she was late. The shopping center had been chaotic. "And the fresh parmesan."

"Great." He set the plates and glasses on their dining room table to her right and then came back and took the grocery bag. When he placed a kiss on her cheek, his beard tickled her face, but she didn't mind. "I'll go cut the bread. They'll be here any second."

Her anxiety mounted, and she took a deep, steadying breath.

He was about to turn around when he paused. "What's wrong?" He knew her better than anyone, and though she was trying to hide her anxiety, she wasn't surprised he could see it.

"Are we doing the right thing?" She lowered her shoulders, and her purse slipped down her arm.

He smiled, his blue eyes sparkling in that charming way of his. After setting the grocery bag down, he reached for her purse and hung it on the coatrack before giving her a hug. "Your brother and niece need help. We have this big old house, with lots of space. We are doing the right thing."

Evelyn took a deep breath, hoping he was right and they wouldn't regret taking her niece in for the next few weeks. Shelby was seventeen and a high school junior in Jacksonville, Florida, and had been suspended from school after a series of mishaps. Evelyn's brother, Eric, was at a loss for what to do with her. He was afraid that if she was home she'd continue to get in trouble with her friends. Shelby was supposed to travel to California next month to live with her mom, so in the meantime, she needed a place to stay.

"We've never raised kids," Evelyn said to her husband, as if he didn't know. "Do we even understand what we're getting ourselves into?"

"No." James smiled. "But she's your niece, and she loves you. Remember when she stayed with us a few years ago? You two had so much fun going to parks and museums. You had a lot in common."

"I remember." Evelyn had loved spending that time with Shelby. "But that was before the divorce and before she started rebelling."

"She just needs to get out of Jacksonville. It sounds like her friends are her biggest problem." James pulled away from Evelyn and grabbed the groceries before walking toward the kitchen again. "Remove her from the problem and she'll be a whole different child."

Evelyn followed James into the kitchen. "But she's not a child anymore. When she was here, she was only thirteen. She's a young woman now."

James set the bread on the counter and pulled out the cutting board. They had recently remodeled their kitchen, and they were still enjoying the newness of the changes they had made. "Don't borrow trouble, Evie. It'll work out. You two will pick up where you left off. She just needs someone to listen and offer her some good advice. It hasn't been easy for her and Eric since Wanda left. And she's probably feeling insecure about moving to California."

No doubt he was right. Wanda abandoned her husband and daughter to move to California with a man she met over the internet. Shelby was devastated but even more so when Wanda refused to take her, hoping to start fresh with her boyfriend. The only reason Shelby was going to California now was because Eric didn't know what else to do. From everything Evelyn had heard, Wanda wasn't happy about the arrangement, but Eric felt it would be best for Shelby. Wanda insisted that they had to wait until next month when she moved into a new apartment.

The doorbell rang, and Evelyn's heart started to pound hard. "They're here."

James chuckled and put his hand on Evelyn's arm. "Relax. Everything will be fine."

"I wish I had a drop of your confidence right now."

"Come on." He winked and took her hand to lead her into the hall.

Evelyn put a smile on her face and touched her hair to make sure there were no silver flyaways sticking up. She wore it at shoulder length, but today, as usual, she had it wrapped up in a twist at the back.

James opened the door.

Eric and Shelby stood on the front stoop.

Evelyn wasn't sure what she was expecting—though she had thought that her brother and niece might offer a smile or two. Instead, both looked like they were in the middle of an intense argument.

"Hi, Sis," Eric said as he stepped into the house with a red suitcase in hand.

"Hi." She hugged her younger brother, noting the extra gray hairs at his temples and the wrinkles around his eyes. He'd lost weight since she'd seen him last year, and there was a hollowness in his eyes she didn't like.

Shelby stood on the stoop, making no move to come into the house, her arms crossed. If Evelyn thought her brother had changed, it was nothing compared to her niece. Gone was the long blond hair she used to wear to her waist, and in its place was a spiked haircut, colored with purple highlights. Her soft, baby-blue eyes, which used to laugh and crinkle at the edges, were now lined in thick black makeup. She wore a pair of blue jeans with more holes than fabric and a black tank top.

It took a second for Evelyn to absorb this version of her niece. It wasn't the new look that bothered her. Her biggest concern was letting Shelby know that she was welcome and wanted. This meeting would go a long way in how Shelby felt about her time in their home, so Evelyn put on a big smile and stepped onto the stoop to give her a hug. "Hello, Shelby."

Shelby stood straight and unbending.

"Welcome back to Charleston," Evelyn said. "I have so many fun things planned for us to do."

"Great." Shelby pulled away from Evelyn's hug but made no move to come into the house.

It wasn't hard for Evelyn to see past the makeup and the hairstyle to the heart of her niece. The previous year had been hard for her and Eric, beyond anything Evelyn could imagine. The abandonment and betrayal they must have felt was overwhelming. Even from a distance, Evelyn had struggled with her own betrayal from her sister-in-law.

"Come in," James said, shaking Eric's hand and smiling broadly at Shelby. "We have supper ready for you."

"Thanks," Eric said, "but if I want to get back to Jacksonville tonight, I should get on the road. I have to work early tomorrow."

"Really?" Evelyn's disappointment was deep. "I was hoping we could visit for a little bit before you had to leave. It's been much too long."

Eric shook his head. "Sorry, Evelyn. I've had a long day, and I had to take off work early to get here. I can't risk being late tomorrow morning."

Shelby rolled her eyes but didn't say a word.

"Here's Shelby's suitcase," Eric said as he set the bag down in the hall. "She refused to pack, so I put things in there that I thought she might need." He opened his wallet and took out a couple of twenty-dollar bills. "If I forgot something, here's some money to pick up whatever she needs."

"No." James pushed the money back toward Eric. "We can take care of it."

Eric tried to give the money to Evelyn, but she also shook her head, so he set it down on the hall table. "Thanks for hanging out with Shelby for a few weeks," he said.

"You mean, thanks for *babysitting* me," Shelby said with attitude.

"We've been over this." Eric sounded exhausted. "You need a change of scenery, and you love Charleston."

"Yeah, when I was a kid." Shelby dropped her arms. "Take me home, *Eric*. You know I don't need a babysitter. This is ridiculous."

"I asked you not to call me Eric. And getting suspended from school four weeks before the end of the semester is ridiculous," he said to his daughter, clearly trying to remain calm. "I've explained to you that your actions have consequences. You don't have a choice this time."

"Like your actions had consequences?" Shelby asked with contempt.

Evelyn took a step closer to James, feeling guilty, though she didn't know why. Was her home a punishment to Shelby? She didn't like that thought at all.

"Whatever." Shelby pushed past her father and finally entered the house. She went to the dining room and sat on a chair, her back toward them.

Eric's shoulders fell, and he turned his tired gaze to Evelyn and James.

"I'm sorry," he said.

"Don't be." Evelyn tried to smile for her brother. "We'll have a good time. You two just need a little space from each other. When you come to pick her up, everyone will have had some time to breathe and reset."

"I hope you're right." Eric glanced into the dining room. "Bye, Shelby."

Shelby didn't respond.

"Call me if you need me," Eric said as he walked back out to the front stoop. "I can be here in less than four hours."

"We'll be fine." James smiled. "Don't worry about us."

"I wish it was that easy."

"Goodbye, Eric." Evelyn followed him outside and gave him another hug, this one tighter than before. "I'm praying for you."

"Thanks. I appreciate all you and James are doing for us."

They pulled apart, and Eric walked down the steps and to the curb, where he had parked his car. "Bye," he called.

Evelyn waved as he got in and pulled away.

She turned back to James, who was standing with her. "Are you still sure about this?" she asked him quietly.

"More now than ever."

"I hope you're right."

But she had a sinking feeling that this wasn't going to be as easy as James thought it was.

Chapter Two

"You need to hurry," Evelyn called to Shelby the next morning as she looked at her wristwatch one more time. "I'm already late, and I have six other people waiting for me to get to work."

"Yeah, yeah." Shelby walked down the steps and into the front hall, where Evelyn was pacing with her work bag over her shoulder. "No one's dying."

Evelyn tried to be patient as she forced herself to smile at her niece. The night before, after Eric left, Shelby had been impossible to talk to. They tried to get her to eat, but she refused. They offered to give her a tour of the house, to show her the work they'd done since the last time she was there, but she sat on the dining room chair with her phone until dark. When it was time to turn in, Shelby didn't even bother to say good night.

Now, as Evelyn caught sight of her, she wanted to groan. Shelby was wearing the same clothes from yesterday. Her eye makeup was smeared almost down to her cheekbones and her spiked hair was lying flat on one side of her head.

"Do you need anything?" Evelyn asked her, wishing Shelby had taken a little more care with her appearance. "A toothbrush? A comb?"

Shelby gave Evelyn a look that could have turned a bucket of water to ice. "What? I'm not good enough for you?"

Evelyn's mouth fell open at the accusation—but wasn't it true? She was going to take Shelby to work with her today, to show her around the new museum and give her a few tasks so she would feel useful. But what would the curators think when Shelby showed up looking this way?

"Fine," Evelyn said, not wanting to waste another minute. "I made some fresh blueberry muffins for you, since I remembered they were your favorite, and got you a glass of milk." She held up the brown paper bag and a to-go cup. "You can eat as we walk."

Shelby eyed the breakfast and wrinkled her nose. "Don't you have coffee around here?"

"I make a cup for myself in the morning, but I didn't know you'd want any. We can get some for you from Joy in the gift shop at the hospital." Evelyn pushed the bag and cup toward Shelby. "We don't have time this morning, but I'll make coffee for you tomorrow. Right now, we need to get moving."

With an eyeroll, Shelby walked to the door and opened it, without taking the breakfast. "I'd rather starve."

Evelyn stared after her but then followed, closing and locking up behind her. James had left earlier that morning, needing to be at the college for a staff meeting. He usually took their car to work, since he had a forty-minute commute. Evelyn was close enough that she could walk to Mercy Hospital. It was one of the reasons she'd originally applied to work there over thirty years ago.

"You didn't eat supper last night," Evelyn said as she caught up to Shelby and handed her the muffins and milk. "I won't send you back to you father looking like a skeleton."

"Whatever. He's shipping me off to California anyway. I doubt he cares what I look like."

"That's not true, and you know it." Evelyn kept up the fast pace with Shelby, thankful that at least they were moving toward the hospital. "I know this has been a tough year for—"

"Don't even start," Shelby said. "I get enough of that from the school counselor. *Poor Shelby*," she said in a high, mocking tone. "*Must be so tough that your mom chose her boyfriend over you. It's normal to feel abandonment and rejection. Just because your mom left doesn't mean you're at fault or that she doesn't love you.*" She rolled her eyes. "Whatever."

Evelyn didn't know how to respond, so she just left the conversation hanging. She and Shelby would have weeks to talk about her thoughts and feelings, but maybe this morning was too early. They needed time to get used to each other again.

At least Shelby took out one of the muffins and ate it.

When they finally arrived at Mercy Hospital, Evelyn didn't even bother to check in at the records department to tell her staff that she was in the building. She was the only person who possessed a set of keys to get into the museum, so she raced toward the entrance, where she found Adam and his team waiting.

"I'm so sorry," she said as she fumbled with her keys to get the door open. "My niece came to visit, and we got behind schedule this morning."

Adam glanced beyond Evelyn and nodded at Shelby, but it was clear that he and the other five curators were irritated at the delay.

Evelyn opened the door, and the team entered the museum, quickly beginning their tasks.

"I'd like to work on the coin display," Adam told Evelyn. "It should be our first priority."

"I agree."

Shelby followed Evelyn to the corner, behind the plastic, where they were storing the coin. For the first time since Shelby had arrived in Charleston, she looked as if she forgot to be mad. Her curiosity was easy to see behind the black makeup, and Evelyn was reminded of her eager enthusiasm to tour museums last time she visited.

Evelyn was going to make a comment but decided to pretend she didn't notice. If she pointed out Shelby's enthusiasm, it would probably vanish.

After setting down his bags and cup of coffee, Adam retrieved the silver case and put on a pair of white cotton gloves. He opened the box and took out the piece.

"What is it?" Shelby asked Evelyn.

"It's a Civil War–era twenty-dollar gold coin," Evelyn explained. She told Shelby the story, enjoying the way Shelby's eyes lit up.

"What kind of a name is Queenie?" she asked with a frown.

"Queenie Bennett was a Southern belle from Mobile, Alabama," Evelyn explained. "Legends say that when she learned about Lieutenant Dixon's death, she died days later from a broken heart. And soon after that, several people in town claimed that her ghost appeared on the Charleston Harbor, late at night, and she could be heard calling for her lost love to return to her."

"Yeah, right," Shelby said.

Evelyn shrugged. "I don't believe in ghosts, but there's a book about all the sightings. They've supposedly been happening since

1864, and the people who claim to see her ghost are pretty adamant about the stories."

Shelby rolled her eyes—something Evelyn was coming to realize was a frequent event—and shrugged. "I'm more skeptical about true love than I am about ghosts."

Adam glanced over his shoulder at Shelby and then at Evelyn and lifted an eyebrow.

It didn't take long to move their supplies to the exhibit floor. Adam had a black cart on wheels, which he used to carry his tools and the artifacts he wanted to prepare.

While he worked and Evelyn supervised, offering her thoughts and opinions, Shelby began to roam about the museum, chatting with the other curators. She asked a lot of questions and then quietly watched.

Many of the artifacts were medical in nature, some with obvious uses, and others so antiquated that they didn't look anything like the modern paraphernalia found in hospitals and clinics.

It did Evelyn's heart good to see Shelby taking an interest in the project, though. Maybe they could still bond over history.

The glass doors opened into the museum and Stacia Westbrook, Evelyn's full-time administrative assistant in records, poked her head into the room.

Adam took notice immediately. He had been bending over the display case but stood up straight and smiled in her direction as he ran his hand over his hair.

Stacia was a pretty young woman, recently graduated from college. She'd been working with Evelyn for over a year, and they got on well. She wore stylish clothes and took extra care with her appearance. Adam wasn't the first young man to fall for her charm.

"I thought I'd find you in here," Stacia said to Evelyn. "Someone is asking to see you."

"Sorry I didn't check in." Evelyn took off the cotton gloves she was wearing. "I was late getting here this morning, and then I got caught up in the installation."

Stacia looked around the room and smiled when her gaze landed on Adam. She was not only pretty, but she was also fun and delightful and was dating someone new every other week. Unfortunately, Adam hadn't had the nerve to ask her out, but Evelyn wouldn't be surprised if he did it soon.

"Shelby," Evelyn called to her niece, "I'm going to run over to records. Would you like to come, or stay here?"

Shelby shrugged. "I'll stay here."

"Okay." Evelyn glanced at Adam. "Is that okay?"

"Of course."

Evelyn had a feeling he'd agree to just about anything she asked him right now.

"Be sure not to touch anything," Evelyn warned her niece.

Shelby didn't bother to respond.

Evelyn left the museum with Stacia and asked, "Who's here to see me?"

"Jerica Dixon." Stacia slipped her long blond hair over her shoulder. "I told her that she could probably find you in the museum, but she said she wanted to talk to you in private first."

Jerica was the Dixon family member Evelyn was eager to meet. They had exchanged several emails and phone calls, but there was nothing quite like meeting in person, especially when they had so much to discuss about Lieutenant Dixon and his connection to the hospital and the exhibit.

"Why does she want to meet in private?" Evelyn asked as they walked into the records department.

"So I can tell you the truth about the gold coin." A woman stood and turned to face Evelyn. She was tall, with rounded features and straight, dark hair. "Everything you've heard about the coin is a lie, and I'm here to set the record straight."

Evelyn stared at the newcomer, too surprised to respond.

"Well," Jerica amended, "at least part of what you know about the coin isn't true." She extended her hand to Evelyn. "I'm Jerica. You must be Evelyn. I'm happy to finally meet you."

Evelyn shook her hand, a little stunned. "I'm happy to meet you too. But you can't leave me hanging. What do you mean about the coin?"

Jerica glanced around the room. A long counter separated the waiting area from the office where Stacia and the others worked. Evelyn's desk was in the center of the room, along one wall. The other was lined with shelves where they kept the older files, which were slowly being converted to digital. Two of the part-time employees, Pam and Rachel, were working on those, while Stacia and the other full-time employee, Jennifer, typed on their computers. At the back of the well-organized records department was a small room which was called the Vault. It was where they kept the oldest files from Mercy Hospital, dating back to the early 1820s, as well as the hospital safe.

"Is there somewhere we can go to talk?" She leaned forward and said in a loud whisper. "*In private*? I don't want anyone to hear what I have to say—yet."

"Unfortunately, I don't have a separate office. Can we speak out in the hall, perhaps?"

Jerica made a face, but then she shrugged. "Sure. I guess so."

"I'll be out in the hall," Evelyn said to Stacia. "And then I hope to take Ms. Dixon to the museum. If you need me, that's where I'll be."

"Sure thing."

Evelyn led Jerica into the hall. It was a busy space, with hospital personnel, salespeople, visitors, and patients walking by. The records department was situated in the Angel Wing, close to the emergency room and not too far from the main entrance. Evelyn directed Jerica to a quiet corner where they wouldn't be overheard.

"What would you like to tell me about the coin?" she asked Jerica.

Jerica looked right and left again. "The coin was stolen from our family," she said in a loud whisper. "And I'm here to get it back."

Evelyn stared at her for a moment, unsure what to say. Was she serious?

"When the submarine was recovered," Jerica continued, "and the coin was discovered with my great-great-uncle's body, our family tried to get it back. The coin belonged to George Dixon, right? And we're the rightful heirs to his property. But a judge decided that the coin was a spoil of war and that it belongs to the United States of America. They took it from us. We've been trying to get them to change their mind since then, but it's expensive."

"I hadn't even considered who would own the property in the recovered submarine."

"They claim the whole submarine is worth forty-million dollars, and it was all given into the care of the state of South Carolina. But if we can prove the coin was the personal belonging of the captain, who *died* serving his country, then why can't it stay in the family?"

"Jerica." Evelyn took a moment to gather her thoughts. "I'm very sorry about your family's troubles. Unfortunately, I don't believe there's anything I can do to help you."

"You don't need to!" Jerica's eyes grew big with excitement. "When the governor comes for the grand opening, I'm planning to be here to make our case. If anyone can help, it's the governor of South Carolina, right?"

"Um." Evelyn didn't know what, if anything, the governor could do—or *would* do—to help. "The governor will be our guest that day, and the last thing I want to do is burden him with this problem."

"You won't have to do a thing." She stood straight and grinned. "I'll do all the talking. I'm good at talking."

Evelyn wasn't sure how to proceed. She had hoped that Jerica would be helpful in answering some of her questions about Lieutenant Dixon, but it appeared that she had her own agenda.

"Is the coin here?" Jerica asked.

"Yes." But Evelyn wasn't comfortable showing it to her now. "It's in the museum."

"Can I see it?"

Evelyn nibbled her bottom lip—but then she noticed a new arrival storming into the hospital.

Jerica must have noticed that Evelyn's attention was stolen, because she turned to look in the direction Evelyn was staring.

Dr. Sarah Langer approached Evelyn, pushing a red dolly in front of her with several large boxes stacked on it.

"Hello, Dr.—"

"Where do you want this stuff?" Dr. Langer asked, her face devoid of emotion.

"In the museum."

"Which way?"

Jerica stared, and Evelyn realized she should probably introduce the two.

"Jerica, this is Dr. Sarah Langer, the executive director of the Charleston Museum. Dr. Langer, this is Jerica Dixon, the great-great-niece of Lieutenant Dixon of the *H.L. Hunley.*"

Dr. Langer's face went from disinterest to complete amazement. "You're related to Lieutenant Dixon? My doctoral thesis was about early submarine warfare, and I did an internship at the Warren Lasch Conservation Center in the early 2000s when they were first starting to preserve the *H.L. Hunley.*"

"Then you know about the coin," Jerica said.

"Of course I do. I was the team member who discovered it."

Jerica's eyes widened. "Can I see it?"

Evelyn indicated that they should follow her. Dr. Langer pushed the dolly, which Evelyn knew held one of the hospital's most prized artifacts: Blackbeard's medicine chest.

They entered the museum, and Evelyn immediately noticed Shelby. She was standing in the center of the room, near the coin display. Adam was nowhere to be seen, and the other curators were busy with their work.

Shelby was holding the coin—without cotton gloves.

"Shelby!" Evelyn shouted her name, and Shelby dropped the coin.

It bounced off the display case and hit the floor, rolling across the carpet and coming to a stop by Jerica's foot.

Everyone stared at the artifact as Adam came out of the plastic area, a frown on his face.

"What were you thinking?" Evelyn asked Shelby as she rushed to put on a pair of gloves, her hands shaking. "No one can touch the coin. I'll put it back."

Jerica started to bend down, but she paused at Evelyn's warning.

"What's going on?" Adam asked.

Evelyn quickly put on the gloves and picked up the coin.

Adam's eyes were huge and his mouth fell open. "Who took the coin out of its case?"

Everyone looked at Shelby.

"What?" she asked.

Slowly, Evelyn walked the piece back to the display and set it on its stand. When it was secure, she turned to Shelby. "I told you not to touch anything."

Shelby rolled her eyes and walked away—not even bothering to apologize or explain herself.

Evelyn's anger burned, but she would have to deal with her niece later. Right now, she needed to do damage control.

"Is this the kind of treatment all the artifacts will get?" Dr. Langer asked. Her red hair was thick and curly. She had it pulled back in a ponytail, but coils had escaped around her face. "Because if you think, for one second, that I'm leaving Blackbeard's chest here under these conditions, you're mistaken."

"My niece is visiting," Evelyn said, trying to keep her cool. "She won't be back in the museum until all the artifacts are secure."

Dr. Langer just shook her head as she crossed her arms. The Charleston Museum recently spent a large sum of money remodeling their medicine wing, and Blackbeard's chest had been their main attraction. It belonged to the hospital and had been on loan at the Charleston Museum for decades. When Evelyn began to recall their items, Dr. Langer had been indignant and difficult to work with. Evelyn understood her frustrations, but there was nothing she could do to make Dr. Langer happy. The medicine chest belonged in the hospital.

"You have our assurance," Adam said to Dr. Langer. "We are being extremely careful with all the artifacts. Unfortunately, I had to step away for a moment and didn't think the coin was in any danger."

"You need to be more careful," she said to him. "These things are irreplaceable."

"I agree." Adam pointed to the boxes. "Is the medicine chest in one of these?"

"Yes. The bottom box." She sighed. "The other two are full of the miscellaneous items that belong to the hospital."

Adam removed the smaller containers and put them on his cart, and then he opened the lowest carton and removed the eighteenth-century medicine chest. It was stained a dark brown and was about two feet long and a foot wide. Bronze metal hinges were rusted with age, but the box was in great shape.

In 1718, the pirate Blackbeard sailed into Charleston with four ships and several hundred men. They took many of the local people as hostages and held them for ransom. It wasn't money or jewels he demanded, but medicine. The governor at the time, Robert Johnson, quickly delivered over four hundred pounds of medical supplies, including this medicine chest, which was believed to have belonged to the governor himself. After receiving the medicine, Blackbeard released the hostages and sailed out of the harbor for good.

Not much later, his ships hit a sandbar near Beaufort Inlet, North Carolina, and were abandoned. Blackbeard died soon after, and the medicine chest was returned to Governor Johnson. His family held on to the chest for several generations, not touching the contents within, and then donated it to the hospital after it was built.

Now, it was back in its rightful place.

"Thank you, Dr. Langer," Adam said. "We will display this proudly."

Dr. Langer pressed her lips together and shook her head. "Hospitals should not be in the business of museum work. What will happen when your curators go back to their offices at the historical society, Evelyn? Will you have a full-time historian here to take care of these artifacts?"

"We will have volunteers handling them," Evelyn said. "Qualified individuals who are thoroughly screened and trained and know what they are doing."

"That's not enough. I have a doctorate in public history. *I* am qualified. Volunteers are not."

"I appreciate your concern," Evelyn said. "But you don't need to worry."

Dr. Langer clicked her tongue. “Rest assured that I will continue to make my feelings about this *museum* known. Don’t be surprised if the hospital administrator decides to close you down when he realizes how woefully unprepared you are for this endeavor.”

Jerica watched with avid interest at the exchanges around her.

Dr. Langer left the museum without another word, slamming through the doors as she left.

“Ouch,” Adam said. “That was painful.” He glanced at Jerica as if seeing her for the first time. “I’m sorry, I don’t think we’ve met.”

“I’m Jerica Dixon,” she said. “And I’ve come to get my family’s gold coin back.”

Evelyn wanted to melt into one of the chairs. She was too tired to deal with all the drama.

Not to mention the emotional confrontation she was soon to have with Shelby.

Chapter Three

It was after five when Evelyn looked up from the coin case display and glanced at the clock. The day had been long but productive. After Jerica left, Evelyn rolled up her sleeves to help the curators wherever possible. Shelby spent most of the day sitting in the corner of the museum with her phone. Evelyn had hoped that Shelby would enjoy spending the day with her, but she would probably be happier staying at the house.

For now, it was time to close up the museum and send everyone home.

"Are you ready to be done for today?" Evelyn asked Adam as he used a special tool to secure the last screw into the display case. The bottom was made of wood, but the top was covered in a clear, plexiglass box. Under the plexiglass, the coin sat on a stand. It was positioned perfectly under a light to showcase its golden shine.

"I think so." Adam set his screwdriver on his work cart. He glanced toward the door. "Do you think Stacia is still here?"

"She usually leaves at five."

The disappointment on Adam's face was so keen, Evelyn said, "But since she's been overseeing the office today, she might still be there."

One by one, the other curators left the museum, but Adam took his time getting his things together.

"You should hurry if you want to try to catch Stacia," Evelyn said.

"Yeah." He put his bag over his shoulder and stared at the door for a second. "It's probably too late. Maybe I'll see if I can talk to her tomorrow."

Evelyn smiled to herself as she gathered together the exhibit floor plans, wondering if he'd ever get up the courage.

"Good night," Adam said as he left the museum.

Before the door closed, Anne was there, wearing a red scarf. She held the door open and smiled at Evelyn. "Can I come in?"

"Of course." Evelyn motioned for her to enter.

"I'm on my way out, but I thought I'd stop by for a second to see how things are going." She glanced around the museum. "Isn't Shelby here? Joy told me she saw her earlier today during lunch."

Evelyn looked in the corner where Shelby had been sitting most of the day, but she was gone. "She was just here." Walking around the museum, Evelyn looked for her niece. "Shelby?"

Anne followed.

They stopped behind a large panel, and Anne said quietly, "How are things going?" Her blue eyes were filled with both understanding and concern. Unlike Evelyn, Anne had raised a daughter and had taken care of her granddaughter. If anyone could understand what today had been like, it was probably Anne.

"It's been a bit rocky," Evelyn admitted. "We need to have a hard conversation later about a couple of things."

Anne nodded, empathy in her kind gaze. "Communication is key. Let her know what your expectations are. It's not easy, but it's necessary."

"I had hoped we could pick up where we left off last time she came to visit, but a lot has changed."

"A girl goes through a lot of growth in her teenage years. Emotionally, mentally, physically. Add to that the trauma of a divorce, and it's no wonder she's hurting. It might take some time."

"I hate wasting that time giving her a lecture, but I don't see any way around it." Evelyn sighed as she glanced around Anne, hoping to see Shelby, but she was nowhere to be found.

"Where did she run off to?" Evelyn asked, almost to herself.

"Do you need help finding her?"

"No. She couldn't have gone far. I had a view of the door all afternoon. If she'd left, I would have seen her. There's not a lot of places she can be hiding in here."

They moved away from the panel, and Evelyn went to the opposite side of the room, where the plastic walls sectioned off a dust-free environment. She pushed aside the opening and found Shelby sitting on one of the stools, Adam's screwdriver in hand.

"This space is off-limits, Shelby."

"I was just curious." Shelby set the screwdriver down. "I'm bored. When are we going to leave?"

"Right now." Evelyn held the flap open.

When Shelby came out, Evelyn said, "This is my friend, Anne."

"Hello, Shelby," Anne said. "You might not remember me, but I met you last time you came to visit your aunt."

"Nice." Shelby's voice was flat. She looked at Evelyn. "I'm starving. Can we get out of here?"

Evelyn glanced at Anne, an apology in her eyes, but Anne shook her head, as if to tell her it wasn't necessary.

"I'll leave you two so you can get to supper." Anne smiled. "I'm sure I'll be seeing you around, Shelby."

After Anne left, Evelyn retrieved her shoulder bag from one of the tables in the plastic area and grabbed her keys to lock the museum.

"James is going to be here any minute to pick us up and take us out for pizza. We're going to one of your favorite pizzerias from your last visit."

"Great."

Evelyn paused as she stared at her niece, tired of her attitude. "Look, Shelby, I'm not your enemy. I was really looking forward to having you visit for a few weeks—and I still am—but for some reason, you're treating me and my friends and coworkers with disrespect. I know you don't want to be here, but could you at least pretend to enjoy yourself?"

"What's the point?" She lifted a shoulder, her black-rimmed eyes looking soulful and depressed.

"If you start acting like you're enjoying yourself, you just might start to have fun."

"Whatever." Shelby absently picked up one of Adam's other tools.

"And please stop touching everything." Evelyn's voice was sharper than she intended.

Shelby dropped the tool on the cart.

Evelyn took a deep breath, trying to calm her emotions. "You should know better—*and* I've told you. These things are rare—like the coin. If something happened to them, there would be no way to ever replace them."

"I got it." Shelby sighed. "Can we go now?"

"I want this to work, Shelby. I really do." Evelyn studied her niece. Despite the frustration, Evelyn's heart was breaking for her. "I know you don't want to talk about your mom, but—"

"There's nothing to say. She left. Big deal."

"It's a very big deal. For all of us. I don't know why she made the choices that led her to California, but I have a feeling something was broken on the inside. And, unfortunately, when people are hurting, they tend to hurt those around them. It's not always intentional, but sometimes they just can't see past their own pain."

"Yeah, well, she seems to be pretty happy there with her boyfriend." Shelby crossed her arms and slouched, not meeting Evelyn's gaze. "She doesn't look as bad off as Eric."

"Why do you call your dad Eric?"

"That's his name, isn't it?"

"What happened to Dad, or Daddy?"

"Why does it matter?"

"Because it's disrespectful and it might hurt him." Evelyn's voice lowered a notch. "And remember what I said before? Hurting people tend to hurt others. In your pain, you might not be noticing that he's pretty miserable too."

"Maybe he should have tried harder to keep Mom."

"You think it's his fault?" Evelyn was trying desperately to understand Shelby's behavior. If she blamed Eric for Wanda leaving, was that why she was so angry and disrespectful toward him?

"I heard them fighting." Shelby lifted a shoulder as if she didn't care, but Evelyn knew she did. A lot. "Nothing he did ever made her happy. She complained constantly. There wasn't enough money, they didn't go out enough, there weren't enough vacations, she didn't like our house, or our car, or Dad's job. And Dad is married to that job. He never left it, even though Mom asked him to look for something different all the time."

"I have a feeling that no matter what your dad did, your mom would have been unhappy."

"Of course you'd take his side." Shelby pushed past Evelyn and walked to the door. "I'm hungry."

Evelyn followed Shelby, turning off the lights, hoping she was saying the right things, though it was difficult to know what to say in a situation like this. She hadn't been there. She didn't know all the ins and outs of her brother's marriage. It wasn't about taking sides, but about helping Shelby navigate the rough waters.

Shelby waited in the hallway as Evelyn locked the doors. She pulled on them to make sure they were secure and then heard her phone ding.

"That's probably James. He said he'd text when he got to the front doors."

Without replying, Shelby started to walk toward the hospital entrance. She didn't look back to make sure Evelyn was following.

When they stepped outside, James got out of the car with a big grin.

It didn't take long for his smile to disappear.

Shelby got into the back seat without greeting him.

"Everything okay?" James asked Evelyn.

"No."

"Rough day?"

"In more ways than one." Evelyn wasn't ready to talk. "I'll tell you about it after we get home."

There was a lot to share with her husband, and, unfortunately, not much of it was good.

The house was quiet as Evelyn tiptoed back up the stairs, not wanting to disturb James or Shelby. It was almost two in the morning, and Evelyn wasn't able to sleep. She had lain in bed for hours, tossing and turning, thinking about Shelby, Jerica Dixon, and Dr. Langer. It was easy enough to push Dr. Langer from her thoughts, since there wasn't much Evelyn could do to make her happy.

But Shelby and Jerica were a different story.

Especially Shelby.

With a glass of water in hand, Evelyn snuck back into her room, closing the door quietly behind her.

"You don't need to worry about waking me," James said as he reached over and turned on his bedside light. "I woke up when you left."

"I'm sorry."

"It's okay." James sat up in bed. "Want to talk about what's bothering you?"

They hadn't had much of a chance after supper, since Evelyn had insisted on taking Shelby to the store to buy her whatever she needed. Her dad hadn't done a great job packing for her, so they purchased all the toiletries a teenage girl would use. Evelyn also bought Shelby a few nice shirts and a couple pairs of pants and shorts.

By the time they got home, there wasn't much time to talk.

Evelyn set her cup down next to her side of the bed and took off her robe. "I'm worried about Shelby. I think her problems are much bigger than I realized."

"It's not your job to fix her." James wore a pair of pajama bottoms and a white T-shirt. His beard was in need of a trim, but he looked handsome, even at two in the morning.

"I know." Evelyn sighed. "I just wish I could do something for her."

"You are. You're loving her and providing her with a safe and comfortable place to stay. Continue to pray for her and speak to her as God leads you."

"I wish I was as good with words as you are."

He grinned. "You don't give yourself enough credit."

"Maybe I'd sleep better if I check on her."

James smiled. "It can't hurt to try."

Evelyn tiptoed out of their bedroom and down the hall. The upstairs was long and narrow, with two bedrooms. Their master suite faced the back courtyard, with a sitting room in the middle and a guest bedroom and bathroom at the front.

Her bare feet didn't make a sound, though the boards creaked each time she took a step.

Shelby's bedroom door was closed, so Evelyn gently turned the knob. What would Shelby do if she woke up and found her aunt peering into her bedroom in the middle of the night? She'd probably run away screaming.

Evelyn peeked into Shelby's room. Everything was so dark it was hard to see—but it was clear that Shelby wasn't in her bed. The comforter hadn't even been ruffled.

"Shelby?" Evelyn asked as she flipped on the light.

The room was empty. Shelby's red suitcase was on the floor, unopened, and the shopping bags from their trip to the store were sitting on the bed, still full.

"Where is she?" James asked as he appeared in the room a few seconds later.

"I don't know." Evelyn went to the bathroom, but it was also empty. "Shelby," she called, louder.

"I'll go check downstairs," James said. "Maybe she's watching a movie."

"I'll look in the basement, though I don't know why she'd go there."

They went down the stairs, James stopping on the main level to check the kitchen and the living room at the back of the house. Evelyn went all the way to the basement. Shelby was nowhere to be found.

Evelyn's anxiety began to rise as she walked back up the stairs. She met James in the front hall.

"The back door is unlocked," he said with a grim face. "It looks like she snuck out."

Groaning, Evelyn went to her purse and pulled out her cell phone. "Where in the world could she have gone? It's not safe to be out on the streets alone this late at night. Anything could happen to her."

"It's not your fault, Evie. Shelby chose to sneak out."

Evelyn found Shelby's phone number and pressed call. It rang several times, and to Evelyn's surprise, Shelby answered.

"What?" she asked.

"Where are you?" Evelyn paced in the hallway, James watching her closely.

"Why does it matter?"

"It matters because you're our responsibility, and it's dangerous out there at this hour."

"I'm fine. Go back to bed."

"Where are you?" Evelyn asked again. "James will come and get you."

"Don't worry about it. I'm fine. I'll come home when I'm ready."

"Shelby, this isn't funny." Evelyn stopped pacing to look out a window, hoping Shelby was in the yard. But it was so dark outside, it was impossible to see. "I want you back at this house right now. We have rules to follow if you want to continue staying here. And one of those rules is that you don't leave the house without telling us—and never in the middle of the night."

"Nothing is going to happen to me."

"You don't know that. If you don't get here in half an hour, I'm calling the police."

"Fine." Shelby ended the call.

Evelyn pulled her phone away from her ear and stared at it for a second. She was shaking. "What have we gotten ourselves into?"

"She said she'll be home within thirty minutes?" James asked, his face serious.

"If 'fine' means yes."

Red crept up James's neck, and his jaw was set in a way that told Evelyn he was angry.

For over twenty minutes, they paced the hall, looked out windows, and kept checking the clock.

Finally, there was a noise on the front stoop, and James went to open the door.

Shelby stood there, in the same clothes she'd been wearing earlier, with the same makeup smeared down her face, only now, it was even more of a mess.

"Where have you been?" James asked.

Shelby looked at him—really looked at him for the first time since she'd arrived.

"I was out." She walked into the house and started to head to the stairway.

"I don't think so." James stepped in her way. "Living room. Now."

Rolling her eyes, Shelby complied with Evelyn and James following close behind.

"Sit." James pointed to a chair.

Evelyn lifted her eyebrows, surprised at her husband's tone. She rarely saw him so upset.

"In this house," he began, "we respect one another. And one of the ways we show respect is we tell each other where we're going and how long we'll be gone. That's just common courtesy. And while you're a guest in our home, you'll abide by our rules. Do you understand?"

Shelby stared at him, her eyes wide. "Yes."

"If you'd like to go back to Jacksonville," Evelyn said, "tell me now and I'll call your dad. We won't force you to stay here if you don't want to be here."

"I don't want to go back to Florida." Shelby looked down at one of the holes in her pants and pulled at a loose string.

"Then don't sneak out again," James said. "We have no tolerance for that kind of thing."

"Okay," Shelby said quietly. "Got it."

"Good." Evelyn glanced at James, and he shared a troubled look with her.

"Can I go to bed now?" Shelby asked.

James crossed his arms. "Do we have your word that you won't leave the house without letting us know?"

"We don't have anything if we don't have trust, Shelby," Evelyn added. "We need to know that we can trust you and that we can rest easy, knowing you'll stay in the house at night."

"You have my word." Shelby stood. "Am I free to leave the living room?"

James sighed. "Evelyn and I want what's best for you, Shelby. We know you're upset, but we don't deserve your disrespect."

"Okay. I got it."

The three of them looked at each other for a moment and then James waved her off.

After Shelby left the living room, Evelyn wilted into a chair. "Where do you think she went?"

"I don't know. But I'm happy she came back."

"Me too." Evelyn tried to smile. "Thanks for talking to her."

"We're in this together, Evie." James put his hand on her shoulder. "Let's go to bed."

Evelyn stood and followed him out of the living room.

She was thankful Shelby was home, but she couldn't shake the fear that there was more trouble coming.

Chapter Four

Evelyn was exhausted on Wednesday morning when she left her bedroom. It had taken her another half an hour to fall asleep the night before, which meant she'd gotten less than four hours sleep. And she would need all the energy she could muster today. There was still work to be done in the museum, but she needed to devote some time to the records department as well. Her responsibilities were piling up there too, and she couldn't put them off for much longer.

Stopping at Shelby's bedroom door, Evelyn knocked. "Shelby?"

There was no answer, so Evelyn pushed open the door, her heart pumping harder. Had Shelby snuck out again?

But Shelby was in her bed, sleeping.

Evelyn relaxed, but then the anxiety returned. She wasn't crazy about the idea of leaving Shelby home alone today, but she couldn't babysit her at Mercy Hospital for the next few weeks.

"Shelby," Evelyn said as she touched her shoulder.

"What?" Shelby groaned. "I'm sleeping."

"I'm leaving for work soon."

No response.

"There are groceries in the kitchen for you, so help yourself. Just clean up when you're done. If you need to leave the house for any reason, please call or text me to tell me where you're going."

"Fine."

"What would you like for supper? If we don't have the right ingredients, I can stop at the grocery store later."

"I don't care."

Evelyn sighed. "Have a good day."

Again, no response.

Evelyn went downstairs and made her morning coffee and oatmeal. James was gone already, having an early-morning class, which left Evelyn alone with her thoughts. She contemplated calling Eric to tell him what had happened but decided to leave it be for now. No harm was done, and if Shelby didn't do it again, then it didn't pay to trouble her dad. He had enough to worry about as it was.

The sky was overcast and heavy with the threat of rain as Evelyn entered Mercy Hospital an hour later. She usually stopped at the gift shop to greet Joy each morning and refill her travel mug with the coffee that Joy kept for the hospital staff, but there wasn't enough time this morning. She didn't want to leave the team of curators waiting for her again.

"Good morning," Evelyn said as she reached the museum's door and found Adam standing there, looking over a file. "I hope you weren't waiting long."

"Just got here a minute ago." He smiled and closed the file.

"Sorry about my niece yesterday." Evelyn slipped the key into the lock. "She's going through a tough time. I had hoped that bringing her to the museum would be good for her, but it didn't work out the way I planned."

"It's fine." Adam put his file into his shoulder bag. "We've all been teenagers."

"You're right." Evelyn appreciated his grace and understanding.

After opening the door, Evelyn flipped on the lights, and Adam went to the workspace in the corner to put down his things.

"If you don't mind," Evelyn called to him, "I'm going to work in Records for a few hours this morning."

He stepped out from behind the plastic wall. "This afternoon we'll need to discuss how we want to display Blackbeard's medicine chest and what items we'll pull out to highlight. If I have any questions before that, I can call or text you."

"Or stop by Records." Evelyn offered a teasing smile. "It'll give you an opportunity to finally talk to Stacia."

A blush crept up Adam's neck as he went to his cart and pushed it to the coin display case. "I don't know if that'll be necessary."

Evelyn chuckled to herself as she went to open the door, but Adam's voice stopped her.

"Evelyn?"

"Yeah?"

"Where's the coin?"

Frowning, Evelyn turned back to look at him. "What do you mean?"

He pointed at the display case, which was empty. "Where's the coin?" he asked again.

Evelyn stared at the empty case for a second and then walked quickly to his side. "It was there last night when I left."

Adam tried to lift the plexiglass lid, but it was still screwed into place. "It's clearly not here now."

"Where could it have gone?" Evelyn swallowed the dread that was climbing her throat.

Without saying another word, Adam rushed over to the plastic wall and pushed it aside. Evelyn followed him. He frantically moved things around, lifting up papers, posters, and other items. He even opened the metal case the coin had come in, but it was nowhere to be found.

"I know it was in the display case last night when I left," Evelyn said. "I watched you screw on the lid with my own eyes."

"Who else was here with you?"

"Anne Mabry stopped by for a second, just after you left, but she was by my side the entire time."

Adam stopped his chaotic search and met Evelyn's gaze. "What about your niece? What was she doing?"

"Shelby?" Evelyn's voice cracked as she said the name. "She was here too."

Except she hadn't been within eyesight of Evelyn the whole time. But the coin had been—at least, it had been for the majority of the time. There were those few minutes when Anne was talking to her about Shelby behind the panel.

"What was she doing?" Adam asked.

"She was on her phone."

"The whole time?"

Evelyn didn't want to incriminate Shelby, but she had to tell the truth. "I did have to go looking for her before I left."

"And?" Adam watched Evelyn closely. "What was she doing when you found her?"

"She was behind the plastic." Evelyn's pulse pounded hard. "With your screwdriver in her hand."

"The one I used to close the case?"

"Yes—but she was just sitting there with it. And she was only out of my sight for a minute or two."

"That's all it takes."

"Are you suggesting she stole the coin?"

"What else could have happened to it?"

"Anything." Evelyn tried to think. "There has to be another explanation."

"Does there?" Adam crossed his arms. "Where is she now?"

"At my house. But the coin was still here when I left last night."

"You remember specifically looking at it right before you walked out?"

Evelyn searched her memory, trying desperately to recall. "I remember looking at it right before you left." Then Anne came in and they talked for a bit, and then she collected Shelby and they went home. "I guess I don't remember seeing it right before I left."

"So the case could have been empty at that point?"

"I don't know." Evelyn put her fingers to her temples.

"All I know is that a very important piece of history is missing, and you and your niece were the last ones to see it."

Evelyn nodded. "You're right. But there has to be some other explanation. I'm going to call Shelby."

Adam scoffed. "Good luck getting the truth out of her."

Ignoring him, Evelyn pulled her phone out of her bag and found Shelby's number. It rang and rang and rang, but Shelby didn't answer.

She ended the call and tried again, walking around the museum, looking all over—though for what, she wasn't certain. The coin couldn't have fallen out of the display case on its own. Someone had deliberately taken it from the case—but who? And how? The only door to the museum was locked tight this morning, and there was no sign of forced entry. There were emergency exit windows, but those were only accessible from the inside, and the seals were not broken. The only person with a key to the museum was herself. The custodial staff didn't even have keys yet.

So who was in the museum last night?

Evelyn ended the call again.

The other curators had arrived, and they were all standing together in a tight circle, speaking in low tones. When Evelyn joined them, they stopped talking and looked at her.

"I told them," Adam said. "No one has any idea what happened to the coin."

"I couldn't get ahold of Shelby, but I will." Evelyn put her phone back in her bag. "I'm going to go talk to security and see if they have video footage of the hallway from last night. If someone broke in, they'll have caught it on the camera."

Adam shared a look of doubt with another curator but didn't voice his opinion.

Evelyn would find the coin and prove to him that Shelby wasn't responsible.

Or was she?

The security office wasn't far from the museum in the Angel Wing. Tucked back into an alcove off the main entrance, it was the hub of all the security cameras in the building. If someone broke into the museum last night, they would have proof of it.

Evelyn greeted Carrie Temple, one of the guards who worked the desk. She was a confident woman with a no-nonsense air about her. She wore her hair back in a tight ponytail and didn't bother with makeup.

"Hello," Carrie said. "How can I help you?"

"I need to look at some security camera footage from last night. One of the artifacts is missing from the museum." At least, she hoped it was just the one thing. She hadn't bothered to check to see if anything else was missing. She'd have to make a note to ask Adam when she returned to the museum.

"Seamus is in his office," Carrie said. "I can see if he has time to look over the footage for you."

"I can ask." Evelyn motioned toward the door that led to the back of the security department. "Mind if I go in?"

"Not at all."

Evelyn walked around the desk and pushed open the door. Though the front desk was in a small alcove, the back of the department was a significant space with dozens of monitors, a couple of desks, and a bunch of knobs, buttons, and levers she'd be too afraid to mess with.

Seamus McCord was the head of security. He could usually be found in his office, but he also took the time to be out and about in the hospital, putting a good face on the department. He was well-known and well-liked among the staff and had helped Evelyn and her friends many times in the past. He was at his desk now, a stack of folders in front of him. He was a tall, muscular man who had been a former deputy sheriff before taking over at Mercy. He didn't look like the desk-job type. Generally, he was in a good mood—but right now, he had a scowl on his face.

"Is this a bad time?" Evelyn asked when she caught his attention.

The scowl disappeared, and Seamus smiled. "No. I just hate reports. The only thing that's worse than reading them is writing them. I always put them off to the last second." He closed the folder and set it to the side. "What can I do for you, Evelyn?"

"One of the artifacts went missing in the new museum. It was there last night when I left, but we can't find it anywhere this morning. The thing is, it was secured under a plexiglass case. I'm wondering if we could look at the security footage from last night to see if anyone broke in."

"Were there signs of a forced entry?"

"No." Evelyn shook her head. "It doesn't look like anyone was in there."

"Who was the last person to see the coin?"

"Me." She quickly explained how she had brought Shelby to work with her and how they had locked everything up before leaving last night.

"Okay." Seamus stood from his desk and went to one of the monitors. "It might take a few minutes for me to bring up the footage."

Evelyn took one of the seats nearby and watched as Seamus used the computer keypad to access the information from the camera outside the museum.

It took a little longer than she anticipated, and she kept checking her phone to see if anyone messaged her. She hoped and prayed that Adam would find the coin tucked away somewhere in the museum—but it didn't seem likely.

"I think I found the footage we're looking for." Seamus enlarged a screenshot and pressed play. "What time did you leave?"

"About five thirty."

Seamus found the image with the time stamp 5:26. Within a couple of minutes, there was Anne, leaving the museum, and a few minutes later, Evelyn and Shelby left. The camera showed Shelby taking off at a fast clip away from Evelyn toward the main entrance.

"Let's fast-forward through the footage," Seamus suggested. "Let me know if you see anything suspicious."

Evelyn watched the monitor closely. The time stamp rolled forward. Six, seven, eight, nine o'clock. People moved through the hallway, but no one even stopped at the glass doors to look inside. Ten, eleven, twelve. The clock turned over to early that morning, but still, nothing. Finally, at two minutes past eight, there was Adam, showing up at the door, and less than a minute later, there was Evelyn.

"Hmm." Seamus leaned back in his chair. "I didn't see anything strange or suspect. Are you sure you didn't notice anyone messing with the artifact before you left?"

"No. I watched Adam secure the lid with a screwdriver, and that was the last I saw the coin."

Seamus tapped his fingers on the tabletop. "I believe you—but, unfortunately, if that coin doesn't show up, we're going to need to question both you and your niece a little more."

Dread pooled in Evelyn's gut at the heaviness in his voice. "Of course."

Seamus sighed. "And I'm going to need to fill out an incident report."

"Sorry."

He chuckled. "It's part of the job, I guess." He rose, and Evelyn did the same. "I'm assuming this coin is valuable."

"Extremely. But its value is more about its significance to history."

"I'm going to have to call the Charleston Police Department. They'll probably send someone over to talk to you and the other museum staff. If the coin doesn't show up before then, we'll discuss the next steps." He lowered his chin and studied Evelyn. "I believe you when you say that you and your niece are innocent, but, unfortunately, this looks pretty incriminating."

Evelyn tried to quell the panic that was starting to get the better of her. "I understand."

"Try to get your niece here, if you can. We'll want to question her too."

"Of course."

"And you said Anne was there shortly before you left?"

"Yes."

"Is she on duty today? Could she meet us in the museum in about thirty minutes? I'll call the police and let them know what's happened."

"I'll find out if she's here. Thank you, Seamus."

"You're welcome. Wish I had better news to share with you."

"I'm happy you're being thorough. I want to find that coin more than anyone else, believe me."

"I do."

Evelyn left the security department.

It was time to call on her friends.

Chapter Five

In less than ten minutes, Anne, Joy, and Shirley were able to gather in the museum, since Evelyn wanted them to look for clues at the place of the crime. A quick text was all it took for them to come to Evelyn's side. Shirley wasn't always able to get away at a moment's notice, but she was on break.

Anne was volunteering on the pediatrics floor. She wore a red shirt and colorful earrings, no doubt to please the children. Her face was a mask of disbelief when Evelyn told her what had happened to the coin.

"Did you see it before you left the museum last night?" Evelyn asked her, hoping and praying her friend could confirm that the coin had been there.

"I'm sorry, Evelyn." Anne shook her head. "I don't remember seeing the coin at all—but I wasn't looking for it. I was more concerned about how things were going between you and Shelby."

"Don't be sorry." Evelyn put her hand on Anne's arm. "We'll figure this out. Someone has to know something."

Shirley was wearing blue scrubs and a cardigan. She was one of few women who could make even boring hospital scrubs look fitted and fashionable. Her thick black hair was pulled back in a simple ponytail, and her cross necklace gleamed under the museum lighting. She glanced at the curators, who were working on other projects around the room. "What about the people who are working with you?" she asked Evelyn. "Would they have any reason to take the coin?"

"Not that I know of." Evelyn clasped her hands together, glancing toward the door to see if the police officers had arrived yet. "None of them has a key to the museum, and the video footage doesn't show anyone breaking in. I have no reason to believe any of them have a motive for taking the coin."

"Who *would* have a motive?" Joy asked. She stood closest to Evelyn, smelling of the scented candles she sold in the gift shop. Her brown hair looked like it had recently been trimmed. She wore it in a bob, tucked behind her ears.

Evelyn shook her head. "There are a couple of obvious people who come to mind, but I don't know how they would have been able to take the coin without being caught on tape."

"Who are they?" Shirley asked. "Maybe, if we can figure out who has a motive, we can narrow down the search and find the culprit."

The museum was cool, for the artifacts' sake. Evelyn wrapped her arms around her waist, trying to get warm. "The first person who comes to mind is Jerica Dixon."

"Who is she?" Shirley asked.

"She's related to Lieutenant George Dixon. She was here yesterday to see the coin and claimed it still belongs to the Dixon family. She hopes to get a chance to talk to the governor when he comes for the grand opening."

"Unless she didn't want to wait for the grand opening," Anne said, "and decided to take the coin without permission."

Evelyn shrugged. “She did seem adamant that the coin belongs to her family.”

The four women were standing near the empty display case, talking quietly.

“Anyone else?” Shirley asked.

“Dr. Sarah Langer comes to mind,” Evelyn admitted. “Though she’s a museum professional and understands the value of an item like the coin.”

Joy stepped closer to Evelyn. “Would she have a motive?”

“She hasn’t been happy about our museum from the beginning,” Evelyn acknowledged. “She was angry about returning the items they had on loan from the hospital, and she said she would continue to let her feelings be known. She said not to be surprised if Garrison closes down the museum after she has a talk with him.”

Garrison Baker was the hospital administrator, and though he was all business, he was also reasonable. He had given Evelyn the go-ahead to get the museum up and running, and she doubted he would stop the production now—but anything was possible.

“I wouldn’t be too worried about Garrison,” Shirley said with a little half smile, revealing her dimples. “I can reassure him that you’ve got everything under control.”

“Do I?” Evelyn had thought so, but the missing coin suggested otherwise.

“Garrison knows you’re more than capable.” Shirley and Garrison had become close in the year that Shirley had been working at Mercy, breaking down the barriers both of them used to guard their hearts. Shirley knew him better than the rest.

"Anyone else you can think of?" Anne asked Evelyn. "Is there another person who might have a reason to take the coin?"

"I can't think of anyone." Evelyn sighed, not wanting to share the next piece of the puzzle but trusting her friends to think the best. "Shelby snuck out of the house last night and didn't come back until almost two thirty this morning."

Joy's eyebrows rose high. "Where did she go?"

"I don't know. She wouldn't tell us anything."

"Do you think she did this?" Shirley asked, watching Evelyn closely.

"I don't think she would—but the truth is, I really don't know her anymore. She was also missing for a few minutes last night while I spoke to Anne, and when I found her, she had Adam's screwdriver in her hand. I didn't bother to look at the coin case before we left, so I can't confirm that it was still there."

"I hate to say this"—Shirley's voice was full of the no-nonsense tone Evelyn had come to appreciate—"but Shelby is probably at the top of our suspect list."

"I tried calling her, hoping she'd come and talk to the police, but she's not answering her phone." Evelyn had also called James to tell him what was happening. He told her that one of his classes was canceled and he'd head home to see if Shelby was there. Maybe she was still sleeping and didn't hear her phone. "James is going to go check on her and let me know if she's home."

"I'm sorry this is happening." Anne put her arm around Evelyn's shoulder. "But don't worry, Evelyn. We'll help you figure this out."

Joy and Shirley smiled and nodded in agreement.

"Thanks. I'm going to need all the help I can get. I haven't called Mr. Lorenzo at the conservation center yet. I'm not looking forward to that."

"I don't blame you." Anne offered Evelyn a sympathetic smile. "I wish we could be more helpful right now."

"The police should be here any minute." Evelyn glanced at the door again. "They'll want to talk with you, since you, Shelby, and I were the last ones here with the coin."

"I'll do whatever I can."

"What about Garrison?" Shirley asked. "Has he been told?"

"Seamus was going to talk to him. I'm expecting to see the two of them any minute."

Right on cue, Seamus and Garrison arrived at the museum. Garrison opened the door and entered. He was a tall man with short black coiled hair laced with silver strands. He wore a dark blue tailored suit and black shiny shoes. When he saw Shirley, he gave her a quick smile before turning his attention on Evelyn.

"Seamus told me what happened," he said to her. "The police are on their way. They've asked that we halt all work on the museum until they can get here and check for clues."

Evelyn glanced at Adam, who had approached.

"Stop working?" Adam asked.

"I'm afraid so." Garrison lifted his hands. "They'll want to search the museum and gather whatever evidence they can find."

"We have a tight schedule," Adam protested. "If we want to be ready for the grand opening, we need to work every possible minute."

"I don't know what to tell you." Garrison shook his head. "It's out of my control."

Evelyn hated to see the project stalled, but the police were right. They needed to comb over the museum to search for any helpful clues.

As Garrison and Seamus spoke to Anne, Evelyn addressed Adam. "Have you had a chance to do an inventory on the other artifacts? Is everything here and accounted for?"

Adam's mouth was pressed into an unhappy line as he glared at Evelyn. "If your niece hadn't been here, none of this would have happened. Why don't you go home and look through her things? Unless she's already hocked the coin."

Indignation rose up in Evelyn's gut. "You have no right to accuse Shelby without proof."

"What proof do I need? She was here, last night, with my screwdriver in her hand when the coin went missing. End of story."

"It's far from the end." Evelyn tried to control her voice, though her anger was mounting with each breath she took. "Shelby didn't take the coin."

"Oh no?" Adam crossed his arms as he stared at Evelyn. "Then was it you? Because you were the last person to see the coin, and you have the only key to the museum."

Evelyn's anger turned to fear as she thought about the repercussions of his accusation. If they didn't find the coin, would she lose her job? Worse—what if Mr. Lorenzo decided to press charges? She'd heard rumors that the coin was worth forty or fifty thousand dollars. She'd be facing a felony charge and jail time if they convicted her.

"I will not lower myself to responding to your accusation," Evelyn said, pulling a bit of dignity around herself. "And I will do everything in my power to find out who the real culprit is. When I do, I think you'll be apologizing for even making such a ludicrous suggestion."

Adam's shoulders softened—only a little—and he took several deep breaths before he said, "I've looked over the collection and don't believe anything else was taken. At this point, it looks like it was only the coin."

Evelyn prided herself on her professionalism, so she chose to put aside Adam's accusation. "Thank you. If you notice anything out of the ordinary, please let me know immediately."

Adam didn't respond but looked to the door at the newest arrivals.

The police had come—and with them, Mr. Lorenzo, his eyes blazing with anger and incredulity.

It was going to be a long afternoon.

A couple of hours later, as Evelyn approached her home, she found herself praying and seeking God for the best way to handle Shelby. With no experience raising children of her own, she wanted to make sure she said and did the right things. She didn't want to hurt her relationship with Shelby or make her niece feel more isolated and abandoned. But how was she going to question her without making an accusation? Because after what Adam said to her earlier, Evelyn knew firsthand how upsetting it felt to be accused of something she didn't do.

Though all of that was second in comparison to what was bothering her now. James had called and said that Shelby wasn't at home—and she still wasn't answering her phone. Evelyn left Mercy soon after the police finished questioning her and Mr. Lorenzo had been assured that they would do everything possible to find the coin. She needed to locate Shelby and put a stop to her disappearing act.

The sky was threatening rain and the air felt thick and heavy as Evelyn walked up the steps and opened the front door. James had offered to pick her up at work, but Evelyn wanted him to be home in case Shelby came back.

"Is she here?" Evelyn asked as she hung her bag in the front hall.

James walked out of the living room at the end of the long hall, his hands in his pockets as he shook his head. "No. And I've tried calling her cell phone more times than I can count. Her suitcase and all of her things are still up in her room, so I would assume she's coming back—but I don't know what to expect."

Evelyn's shoulders fell. "What are we going to do? The police want to talk to her as soon as I can get her to the station. The longer it takes, the more incriminating it becomes."

"I don't know, Evie, but something has to change. We can't let her get away with this over and over again."

"You should get back to campus." Evelyn met her husband in the middle of the hall, feeling horrible that he had made the forty-minute commute for nothing. "You have a class to teach, don't you?"

"I do. But I don't want to leave you here alone to deal with this mess."

"I can handle it." Evelyn put a smile on her face to show her husband she was more than capable. "Go, or you'll be late."

He gave her a quick kiss and then left through the back door.

Evelyn hadn't eaten since breakfast, and she could use something in her stomach—especially because she still needed to call her brother and tell him what had happened. Would he be disappointed in Evelyn? She felt like she had not only failed Shelby, she had failed her brother. Shelby was missing again—and the police were waiting to question her. Not exactly a stellar second day on the job.

James pulled out of the driveway as Evelyn stood at the sink and filled the teakettle. She might not be able to eat something, but at least she could drink some tea to help calm her nerves.

She was grabbing a tea bag when she heard the front door open.

"Shelby?" Evelyn dropped the tea bag on the counter and went into the hall.

Shelby was standing near the door in a pair of shorts and a T-shirt that Evelyn had purchased for her the night before. She had showered, and her face was free of makeup. The purple streaks in her hair must have been temporary, because they were gone and so were the spikes.

With her natural, short blond hair and beautiful blue eyes without makeup, Shelby looked younger and more vulnerable.

"Where have you been?" Evelyn asked, relieved to see Shelby and angry that she hadn't answered her phone.

"I walked around the historic district to check it out." Shelby closed the door and headed toward the stairs.

"Hold on," Evelyn said. "We need to talk."

Shelby rolled her eyes. "Not this again. I texted you and told you where I was going. I don't need another lecture."

"When?" Evelyn asked. "I didn't get a text from you."

"I sent it to you like twenty minutes after you left today."

"I didn't get it."

Shelby shrugged. "Well, I sent it."

"Why didn't you answer your phone? James and I have been trying to get ahold of you for hours."

She pulled her phone out of her back pocket and held it up. "It died right after I left the house. I forgot to charge it last night."

The screen was black, and Shelby touched it a couple of times to show Evelyn that it wouldn't turn on.

All the bluster left Evelyn, and she felt weak and exhausted. Had she missed Shelby's text in all of the commotion earlier today? Evelyn walked to the front door and pulled her phone out of her bag. She touched her texting icon and, sure enough, there was a text from Shelby from a few minutes after eight.

"See?" Shelby said.

Evelyn set her phone on the hall table and turned back to her niece. "I'm sorry, Shelby. I don't know how I missed the text."

"Whatever." Shelby started to walk toward the stairs, but Evelyn stopped her again.

"We still need to talk about something else. Do you want to join me for tea?"

"Um, no." Shelby lifted an eyebrow. "Gross. I don't drink tea."

Evelyn motioned for her niece to follow her to the kitchen. "Well, I do."

Shelby begrudgingly entered the kitchen and took a seat on one of the stools.

The kettle was steaming, though it hadn't started to whistle yet. Evelyn took it off the heat and filled a cup, then set her chamomile tea bag inside. The earthy scent spiraled up and filled Evelyn's nose.

There was no reason to delay telling Shelby about the coin, so she jumped right in. "Do you remember the coin in the museum yesterday? The one you were holding when you shouldn't have?"

"Yeah." Shelby's blue eyes were clear as she stared at Evelyn.

"It's missing." Evelyn sighed. "When I got to work today, it wasn't in the display case, and we can't find it anywhere."

"So?"

"So, there are a lot of really upset people. The coin is irreplaceable, and you and I were the last two people to see it."

Shelby sat up straighter. "What are you saying?"

"I had to talk to the police today, and they want to talk to you too."

"I'm not talking to any police."

"You don't have much of a choice. They want to know if you remember seeing anything suspicious yesterday."

"Do they think I took it?" Shelby's back was now rigid as she stared at Evelyn.

"I really don't know. I'm the only person with a key, and no one else entered the museum last night."

"So they think you did it?"

"They don't have enough evidence to know who is responsible."

"It wasn't me." Shelby shook her head. "I couldn't care less about that coin."

"Unfortunately, you were holding the tool used to get into the display case, and you weren't home last night. When they asked me,

I had to be honest, and I told them that you refused to tell me where you were. That doesn't look good, Shelby."

"I didn't go to the hospital, if that's what you think." Shelby frowned at Evelyn. "I wasn't even near the hospital."

"Then where were you?" Evelyn pleaded with her eyes, hoping Shelby would finally tell her the truth.

"I was out walking around," she said. "I didn't really go anywhere. Just wandered around the streets."

"Do you know how dangerous that is? You could have been mugged—or worse."

"I didn't even see anyone. The streets were quiet."

"This explanation doesn't offer you an alibi. The police will want to know if you saw anyone who could identify you and put you somewhere other than the hospital."

Shelby shrugged. "Sorry."

"No, I'm sorry, Shelby." Evelyn's heart was heavy. "Maybe staying here isn't such a good idea. Like James said last night, if we can't trust each other, then this isn't going to work."

"But I told you the truth! I wasn't at the hospital last night. And today, I texted you and told you where I was going to be." Her voice rose with each word she spoke. "I want to stay here, Aunt Evelyn. I don't want to go back home."

Evelyn leaned against the counter as she studied her niece. Shelby's plea felt authentic—and she had done as Evelyn and James had asked. Maybe sending her away wasn't a good idea right now. Among other reasons, it might make her look guilty.

"You believe me, don't you?" Shelby asked. "I didn't take the coin. You can look through my things if you want."

"I'm not going to look through your things." Though the idea had crossed Evelyn's mind. But trust was a two-way street. Shelby needed to trust Evelyn to give her space and privacy.

"I wouldn't do something like this," Shelby said. "I know how much the museum means to you."

"I do believe you, Shelby. But I'm afraid I'm still going to have to take you to the police department so they can talk to you. We need to cooperate as much as possible." Evelyn hated to subject Shelby to questioning, but they needed to know what happened to the coin. Even if she hadn't taken it, maybe Shelby had noticed something that the others hadn't.

"Fine." Shelby crossed her arms—and though she agreed, she didn't look happy.

Chapter Six

On Thursday morning, Evelyn entered Mercy Hospital feeling energized and ready to find the coin. She was so tired yesterday after taking Shelby to the police station that she crashed into bed shortly after cleaning up supper and didn't wake up until her alarm clock went off. She hadn't even stirred when James came to bed.

Now, as she walked through the main entrance, she braced herself for whatever she would face today. The police had been kind to Shelby the day before, but she wasn't able to give them any more information than Evelyn had. And after searching through the museum and finding no clue, they weren't any closer to nabbing the culprit. Evelyn assured them that she would cooperate with their investigation, and secretly, she had started to plan her own. With help from Joy, Anne, and Shirley, she was confident they could figure this thing out.

It was still early, so Evelyn stopped by the hospital gift shop to refill her travel mug with coffee.

Joy was standing behind the cashier's counter, her phone in hand, as she watched something on the screen. Whatever it was, it had her completely captivated. She didn't even notice Evelyn's entrance until Evelyn was standing directly in front of her.

"Oh!" Joy startled and put her hand up to her heart. "You scared me."

"Sorry." Evelyn couldn't help but smile at Joy's reaction. "I wasn't trying."

The gift shop was such a charming space in the hospital. It was full of all sorts of fun gifts, beautiful housewares, and scented candles. There was a cooler with fresh-cut flowers, some that Joy brought from her own garden, and a display rack of thoughtful and funny cards. One shelf was lined with used books, which Joy allowed people to trade or borrow. The shop was a perfect reflection of Joy's caring and organized personality.

The scent of fresh-brewed coffee called to Evelyn, and she went to the pot, which Joy kept warm at all times.

Evelyn was refilling her mug when Joy said, "Have you seen the video?"

"What video?"

Joy came around the counter, her phone in her hand. "I was watching it again when you came in."

"Again?" Evelyn finished filling her mug and gave Joy her full attention. "What kind of video?"

"It was captured last night on Charleston Harbor." Joy tapped her phone's screen a couple of times and then turned it to face Evelyn. "The video has gone viral since it was posted early this morning. Take a look and tell me what you see."

Joy watched Evelyn as the video began to play.

It was dark, but it was easy to make out the lines of Charleston Harbor. Waves crashed against the cement seawall lining the shore, and at the top of the wall, where the sidewalk allowed people to look out at the harbor, a lone figure walked. Though it appeared to be a woman, it was too far away to discern any other details. She was wearing a flowing gown, and her long hair was blowing in the wind as she called out to sea. It was hard to make out what she was saying, but it almost sounded like she was calling for someone named George.

But just like that, she disappeared! The video continued to roll for a few seconds, and whoever had caught it on video exclaimed their shock and amazement. It sounded like a man, and he could be heard saying, "What in the world was that?"

Then the clip ended.

"I've watched it several times this morning," Joy said. "People are claiming it's Queenie's ghost."

"Queenie's ghost?" Evelyn frowned. "As in, Lieutenant George Dixon's sweetheart?"

"Exactly. Even the author of the book about the sightings, Clement Hawk, chimed in and left a comment on the video. He said it's consistent with the other times. Queenie is there, calling out for George, and then she disappears in the next heartbeat. He plans to keep this incident on file to add to the next revision of his book."

"That's ridiculous," Evelyn said, pursing her lips. "I don't believe it's true for a second."

Joy shrugged. "Neither do I, but a whole bunch of people do, and they're excited."

"I'm sure they are." Evelyn shook her head in wonder. "Thanks for the coffee. I hate to run, but I need to make an appearance in Records before I open up the museum for Adam and his team."

"No worries. Let me know when you take your lunch break and I'll join you, if you'd like."

"Absolutely."

Evelyn left the gift shop and entered the records department. Stacia was already there. She had been such a big help to Evelyn since the museum project started, taking over many of the responsibilities that usually fell on Evelyn's shoulders.

"Good morning," Evelyn said as she walked around the front desk.

"Oh, hi." Stacia turned away from her computer and handed Evelyn a note. "Hunter called this morning and would like you to return his call if you have a minute."

Hunter O'Reilly was a newspaper reporter for the *Charleston Times*. Evelyn had met him several months before when he did a story on a special ring that came into Mercy Hospital. At the time, Hunter and Stacia started to date, but the pair went out only a few times.

"Did he say what the call was about?" Evelyn took the note and looked at the number.

"It sounds like he wants to interview you about the missing coin."

"Has news spread so quickly?" Groaning, Evelyn went to her desk and took a seat. "I thought we'd have a little more time to figure this out before the public became involved. The last thing I want is for the museum to get a bad reputation."

Stacia shrugged. "It might be bad publicity, but at least it's still publicity. Just think of all the people who will learn about the new museum because of this. Hunter actually asked me if this was a publicity stunt."

Evelyn opened her eyes wide. "Who would do something like that?"

"Who has the most to gain from this museum being a success?"

"I do." Evelyn paused as she stared at Stacia. "Do people really think I would do this for publicity's sake?"

"It was just something Hunter mentioned in passing. I don't think people are really suspecting you of stealing the coin."

"Unfortunately, there are a few people who have accused me already."

It was Stacia's turn to look shocked. "If anyone truly knew you, they would never suggest such a thing."

"I appreciate your vote of confidence." Evelyn took a deep breath. "I should probably call Hunter right away to set the record straight before he prints something that will hurt the museum."

"Hunter is always looking for the truth," Stacia assured her. "He'll believe you."

"Thanks." Evelyn lifted her phone and typed in Hunter's number.

Records was quiet this early in the morning. Stacia and Evelyn were the only ones in the office, which Evelyn appreciated for this call. She had no desire for her other staff members to be privy to all the rumors.

"This is Hunter O'Reilly."

"Hello, Hunter, this is Evelyn Perry."

"Hi, Mrs. Perry! Thanks for calling me back so quickly."

Evelyn could imagine Hunter's black horn-rimmed glasses and his fifties-inspired hairstyle and clothes. He was a charismatic man and a great reporter. "Stacia told me that you heard about the coin."

"I did—but, better yet, I also heard about the Queenie Bennett sighting."

Evelyn wasn't sure how the two connected. "Can I help you with something?"

"I heard that Lieutenant Dixon's coin went missing in the museum the night before last, and then I heard that Queenie Bennett's ghost was seen on the harbor last night, calling for her long-lost sweetheart. Don't you think that's a strange coincidence?"

"I don't know what to think about it."

"There's a rumor going around that the coin just disappeared into thin air. No one was seen entering or exiting the museum, and the coin display case was still screwed shut, but the coin was gone. Is that true?"

"It's true that no one was seen entering or exiting the museum and that the case was still intact—but I hesitate to say the coin disappeared into thin air. Someone had to have taken it."

"Some people think Queenie's ghost took it. And just like she disappears on the video, she made the coin disappear. What do you think of that?"

"I think this is poor reporting, Hunter. I don't believe in ghosts, and I don't believe in anything disappearing into thin air."

"I would tend to agree with you," Hunter said. "But there's a lot of hype this morning about the sighting and the missing coin—and it's still early. Just imagine how much more this story will spread as the workday progresses. I'm planning to write up an article online to get people to click over to our newspaper. I'll give the details about the stolen coin—and the real history of Lieutenant Dixon and Queenie Bennett—but I am also going to talk about the strange sightings and the mysterious way the coin disappeared."

Evelyn sighed. Maybe this would ultimately work in her favor. If the public read that the coin was stolen by an ethereal being, then maybe it would take the suspicions and accusations off her shoulders until she could get to the bottom of this mystery.

"Is there something I can help you with?" Evelyn asked Hunter. "Any information I can offer?"

"You already have. You confirmed that the coin has disappeared without a trace. That's all I was after. Mind if I quote you?"

"I wish you wouldn't." The less her name was connected to the story, the better.

"You got it. Thanks for your help, Mrs. Perry."

"Goodbye, Hunter."

He hung up, and Evelyn set her phone down.

As she thought about the strange sighting of Queenie Bennett, she couldn't shake the thought that maybe there was some connection between her and the coin. Not in the way that Hunter was suggesting but in a more tangible light.

"Stacia," Evelyn said, "can you find me a number to contact Clement Hawk, the author of the Queenie Bennett book? I'd like to chat with him."

"Absolutely."

Evelyn wasn't sure what she would find, but she needed to make certain she had every possibility covered.

And as soon as she had the time, she'd contact Jerica and Dr. Langer. She wasn't convinced that they weren't involved.

Between her work in the records department and helping in the museum now that the police had released the crime scene and allowed the curators back in to work, Evelyn's morning went by in a blur. She hadn't even had time to stop and think much about the coin, let alone make a few phone calls to touch base with Clement Hawk, Jerica, or Dr. Langer.

But it was lunchtime, and Evelyn was starving. She sent a text to Joy, who said that Anne and Shirley would meet them out in the Grove for lunch.

Evelyn stopped into the coffee shop in the corner of the main entry, grabbed a Mediterranean salad and a glass of sweet tea, and then left the building to join her friends outside.

The beautiful green space was a parklike setting amid the large wings of Mercy Hospital and the businesses lining Tradd Street. A series of pathways led from each building, and to the south, closest to the original entrance of the hospital, stood the Angel of Mercy statue. Gorgeous rose beds offered vibrant colors and smells in the summer months, and the green grass was a stunning contrast to the brick buildings.

Evelyn's friends were already seated at one of the concrete tables, under a large umbrella to protect against the bright sunshine.

"Hello," Evelyn said as she set her lunch down on the table. She took a seat and sighed with a bit of relief for this break and a chance to be with her friends. The ocean air felt refreshing.

"You look exhausted," Shirley said as she moved aside her soda to give Evelyn a bit more space. "Any new leads on the coin?"

"I wish I had more to report." Evelyn took the lid off her salad. "I've been so busy this morning, I haven't had time to do any more investigating."

"You heard about the sighting of Queenie Bennett's ghost last night, right?" Joy asked Shirley.

"I heard something," Shirley said. "But I didn't give it much thought."

"Neither did I." Anne sighed. "Probably someone trying to play a prank while Lieutenant Dixon is on everyone's mind."

"The *Charleston Times* called today," Evelyn told her friends about her conversation with Hunter as she inspected the salad she had purchased. It was loaded with vegetables and had a side of vinaigrette. "I agree with all of you. This isn't a ghost sighting, but I am curious to talk to the author of the Queenie Bennett book to see what he thinks."

"I'd love to talk to him too," Joy said. "All of this fascinates me."

"I'm going to call and set up an appointment," Evelyn said to Joy. "Do you want to come with?"

"Sure."

"Evelyn?" Evelyn looked up to see Jerica approaching their table. "You're just the person I was coming to see."

Evelyn smiled when Jerica sat down beside her. She said, "Jerica, these are my friends, Shirley Bashore, Anne Mabry, and Joy Atkins."

Jerica nodded at each person.

"Ladies," Evelyn said to her friends, "this is Jerica Dixon. She's come to Charleston because of the coin."

"Which is the reason I'm here today." Jerica turned to address Evelyn. "The friend I'm staying with just showed me an article from the *Charleston Times*. It said the coin vanished. Is that true?"

"Unfortunately, it is true."

"Why didn't you call me?" Jerica frowned. "Why'd I have to find out about it from the internet?"

"I'm sorry." Evelyn tried to move over on the bench a little more, but there was no room. "I've been so busy, I didn't have a chance."

"Didn't you think the rightful owner of the coin should be notified immediately?" Jerica crossed her arms. "I thought we were friends, Evelyn."

Anne, Shirley, and Joy sat quietly. Joy looked like she wasn't trying to pay attention, and Anne fiddled with her sandwich wrapper. Shirley was the only one openly watching.

"Again," Evelyn said to Jerica, "I'm sorry I didn't call you. I know you have a connection to the coin, but we don't know if you're the rightful owner. I've been busy trying to handle the situation. As you can imagine, it's been a bit difficult."

"What are we going to do about this?" Jerica looked around the table. "What's our plan of action? How are we getting the coin back? Who are our suspects? Why are we just sitting here?"

"The police have been informed," Shirley answered for the rest of them. "They're doing the official investigation."

Jerica frowned. "You know how that's going to go. They'll sit on this thing for years. We need to take matters into our own hands."

"I think we have things well under control at this point," Evelyn said, though she didn't quite believe it herself. Jerica was one of their prime suspects, and Evelyn wanted her to trust that they were competent. "I was planning to contact you sometime today, though."

"Really? Why? Do you have something I can do to help?"

"I was going to ask you where you were the night the coin went missing." Evelyn watched Jerica closely to see if the question upset her.

"Two nights ago?" Jerica closed one eye as she thought. "Easy! My friends took me to Sullivan's Island Lighthouse. We stayed there in an old bed-and-breakfast."

"The whole evening?"

"Yep."

"Do you have a witness to verify your whereabouts?"

"Sure." Jerica looked at Evelyn out of the corner of her eye. "Do you think *I* took the coin?"

"You're one of the few people who might have had a motive. I don't mean to accuse you—"

"It's okay." Jerica straightened her back. "I've never been part of something like this before. It's kind of like being in a movie. Exciting and a little dangerous."

Evelyn shared a glance with her friends. This experience didn't feel exciting to her at all. She wished it had never happened and that they could find the coin and get on with their lives.

But one look at Jerica, who was beaming, indicated that she was *enjoying* this.

"So where do we start?" Jerica asked Evelyn. "Do we have a list of suspects compiled? Do we make them take lie detector tests? Follow them and sneak into their homes to search for the lost coin?"

"No." Evelyn gave her head a decided shake. "We will do none of those things." Concern tightened her brow. "Jerica, it's important that we leave this case up to the police. There's not a lot you can do to help at this point."

Jerica pursed her lips and said, "Hmm. Well, that's a bummer."

"If I think of anything that you can do," Evelyn said, "I'll be sure to call you."

"Really?" Jerica's face brightened. "You promise?"

"Yes, of course."

"Great. I'll be waiting for your call." Jerica sighed. "Well, I suppose I should mosey on by then. I was thinking about heading over to the harbor to see if I could find any clues there from Queenie's ghost sighting. If I learn something new, I'll call you, Evelyn."

"I appreciate that."

"Bye!" Jerica waved at all of them, turning back a few times to wave again as she walked away and disappeared around the side of the building.

"Did you notice how excited she got about the whole thing?" Shirley asked. "Do you think she took the coin for the drama?"

"I don't know what to think." Evelyn took her vinaigrette packet and opened it. "What I do know is that Jerica Dixon believes the coin is rightfully hers and so she had motive to take it. But if she was at Sullivan's Island, then she couldn't have. I'm at a loss."

Anne touched Evelyn's arm in solidarity, and Joy said, "We'll figure it out."

"Thanks." Evelyn was no closer to knowing who took the coin, but she was hopeful that they would put all the pieces of the puzzle together before the grand opening.

They had to.

Chapter Seven

IT WASN'T UNTIL LATE THE next afternoon, Friday, when Evelyn and Joy were able to visit with Clement Hawk. He was an elderly man who lived in a historic home on East Battery Street, facing Charleston Harbor. The address wasn't far from Mercy Hospital, so Evelyn and Joy walked there together after work.

"I had no idea Mr. Hawk lived in such a fine home," Joy said as she looked up at the three-story mansion.

The white stucco building was a Charleston Single House, though much bigger than Evelyn's. Like many homes on the peninsula, the lowest piazza had been enclosed, while the two upper-level piazzas were open, allowing for breathtaking views of the harbor and the coveted ocean breeze. Black shutters flanked each window, the most prominent being a three-level bay looking toward the water.

"I had a cousin who toured one of these houses when they were for sale," Evelyn said as they approached the front door. "They sell for upwards of five to ten million dollars here on Battery Street."

"I can see why." Joy's eyebrows rose high on her forehead. "Weren't most of them built pre-Civil War?"

"They were. Just up the street, at the Edmonston-Alston Home, General Beauregard, the Confederate Commander who gave orders to fire on Fort Sumter, stood on the piazza to watch the action. All of these houses have stood the test of time to tell their tales."

Evelyn checked the address on the piece of paper Stacia had given her one more time and then rang the doorbell.

"Do you know anything about Clement Hawk?" Joy asked as they waited.

The air was humid and warm, and the gentle smell of the ocean brushed past Evelyn as she shook her head. "Not a lot. I remember when he released the Queenie Bennett book a few years ago. There was a little stir about it, but its value only lies here in Charleston, so it didn't make a big splash. If I remember correctly, he's a bit of a recluse and the heir to an ancient indigo fortune."

"If he's a recluse, I'm surprised he agreed to meet with us."

"I told him I was the project manager for the Mercy Hospital Museum and I was the last person to see Lieutenant Dixon's coin. I think that was enough to pique his interest."

"Ah." Joy smiled.

After a few moments, the front door opened. Clement Hawk was older than Evelyn had expected, with thinning white hair, age spots on his face and scalp, and gnarled hands. He was a tall, thin man, but time had bent him over and he walked with a cane.

"Mrs. Perry and Mrs. Atkins, I presume?" he asked in a cultured Southern drawl.

"I'm Evelyn Perry," Evelyn said, "and this is my friend Joy Atkins. It's so nice to meet you, Mr. Hawk."

"The pleasure is mine. Won't you come in?"

They entered the foyer, and it was as grand on the inside as it was on the outside. A beautiful open staircase graced the front hall, while marble floors and intricate woodwork spoke of a wealth and lifestyle that defied Evelyn's imagination. She could almost see the extravagant balls and soirees this home must have hosted over the years and wondered at the occupants that had lived there.

"Please," Mr. Hawk said as he indicated the front parlor, "have a seat. My housekeeper is bringing us a tea tray."

Evelyn felt a little self-conscious as she and Joy entered the parlor. Her simple slacks and blouse didn't feel quite up to par with the elaborate surroundings. The room was bright and airy, with a towering ceiling, crystal chandeliers, and floor-to-ceiling windows overlooking the sparkling harbor.

"I would suggest we take our tea on the upper piazza," Mr. Hawk said as he slowly followed them into the parlor, "but the stairs don't agree with me. I haven't been upstairs in years."

"This is just fine," Evelyn assured him. "You have such a beautiful home."

"Thank you. I've lived here all my life, and my daddy before me, and his daddy before him, and so on. It's been in the family since it was built in 1837. Most of the furnishings are original and added to over the years by each family member."

The furniture was delicate and old. Evelyn was afraid to take a seat, but he indicated that they should sit. Evelyn chose an armchair with a rose brocade, while Joy sat on the chair that matched.

Mr. Hawk took a seat on the sofa facing them. The ornate fireplace to his left was unlit, and so clean that Evelyn wondered if it was ever used.

"I believe I know why you've come," Mr. Hawk said to the ladies, "so perhaps we can dispense with the formalities and get down to business."

"If that's what you'd like." Evelyn longed to know what he could tell her about Queenie, but she was also fascinated by his home and his family history. It was one of the downfalls of loving history—being easily distracted.

"Have you seen the video of the alleged sighting?" Joy asked Mr. Hawk.

"I don't believe it was 'alleged,' as you claim." Mr. Hawk crossed his legs and put his hands in his lap. "It was Queenie."

Evelyn leaned forward. "How can you be so sure?"

Mr. Hawk lifted his hand. "I've seen her myself."

Joy and Evelyn looked at each other, and then Joy said, "You have?"

"That's why I wrote the book, you see? I've lived on the harbor my whole life, and the first time I saw her ghost was when I was just five years old. It was late, and I was supposed to be asleep, but it was such a hot and sultry night that I snuck out onto the topmost piazza. She walked along the harbor wall, her hair and dress blowing in the salty sea air, calling out George's name in a low lament. I had no idea who she was or why she was there. But then she disappeared. The next morning, when my nanny found me sleeping on the piazza, I told her what I had seen, and she said it was Queenie Bennett, come to find her long-lost love." He shook his head, his gaze far-off, as if he were seeing a different time and place. "I've seen her two other times in my ninety-seven years, and both instances she looked the exact same. When I saw the video yesterday, I knew immediately it was the apparition I've seen before."

"What about the other reports you wrote about in your book?" Evelyn asked. "Surely you're not the only person who claims to have seen her."

"Of course I'm not. The sightings began in the late 1860s, soon after Queenie died of a broken heart. I have found over a hundred reports claiming people have seen her—including those from my own family. And not just here on the harbor but throughout historic Charleston. Even near Mercy Hospital. Some people claim that she's looking for Lieutenant Dixon and has been to the hospital, the jail, Fort Sumter, and more."

"Mercy Hospital?" Evelyn asked, a shiver running up her spine, despite her lack of belief in such things.

"When Lieutenant Dixon left Queenie in Mobile to bring the *H.L. Hunley* to Charleston," Mr. Hawk explained, "she was only seventeen years old. Her love was innocent and pure, and she truly believed it was invincible. Nothing could stand in their way. After all, the twenty-dollar coin she had given him saved his life at the Battle of Shiloh. Over a third of Lieutenant Dixon's regiment died that day—but he was spared. Imagine how she felt, when just two years later, his submarine didn't resurface after engaging that Union battleship. She had to believe that her love for him would somehow find another way. Her hope refused to sink with her beloved."

"The story is remarkable," Evelyn agreed. "But many people have lost their true love. Why do people in Charleston think this case is so special?"

"Who can say?" Mr. Hawk asked, his eyes filling with sadness. "The story becomes even more tragic when you learn that Queenie died soon after she realized George wasn't coming back. Perhaps their love was made of something greater than we can imagine."

A middle-aged woman entered the parlor carrying a tray laden with teacups, a teapot, cream, sugar, and delicate little sugar cookies. She had a kind face and a quick smile. When she set the tray down, she offered to serve the women and then Mr. Hawk. Finally, she said, "Will you be needing anything else?"

"No, thank you, Helen," Mr. Hawk said with a gentle smile.

She winked at him and then laid a gentle hand on his shoulder before leaving the room.

Evelyn's cup steamed in her hand, offering a tendril of blueberry aroma. She tried to enjoy the simple pleasure of taking tea in such a fine home, but she couldn't let the matter of Queenie Bennett rest. After all, that was why they'd come. "Have there ever been cases of people *pretending* to be Queenie Bennett?"

"Why would someone want to do that?" Mr. Hawk asked, his expression truly perplexed.

"For a joke, or to trick people, I suppose."

"That's ridiculous." Mr. Hawk shook his head. "I don't think that's very nice."

"You don't believe that some of these sightings could be people playing pranks?" Joy asked their host. "Or lying?"

"For what purpose?" Mr. Hawk asked.

"Attention?" Evelyn suggested. "Or distraction. Is it possible that whoever took the coin from the hospital museum might be distracting people with this so-called 'appearance'?"

Mr. Hawk lowered his teacup and tilted his head, as if he had never considered such a thing. "I suppose it's possible." His eyes were troubled as he looked between Evelyn and Joy. "To those of us who have seen Queenie with our own eyes, it seems a cruel joke to imitate her."

It was clear to Evelyn that whatever Mr. Hawk had experienced was deeply personal and something he took very seriously. She hated to destroy his tenuous reality.

"You've never come across instances in which the sighting turned out to be a prank?" Joy asked again. "Not once out of a hundred reports?"

"Of course I have," Mr. Hawk said, "but then I don't claim those as real reports. The one hundred that I have gathered are authenticated."

"How are they authenticated?" Evelyn asked.

"By me, of course." Mr. Hawk lifted his wrinkled chin. "I'm the foremost authority on Queenie Bennett's ghost, and I am the only person qualified to authenticate the sightings."

"And this most recent one?" Joy asked.

"It's real." He nodded once, as if to put a period on the end of his statement.

How could Evelyn debate with that?

An hour later, Evelyn and Joy left Mr. Hawk's home, knowing a lot more about the history of the house, his family's connection to the indigo trade, and little tidbits about his life in Charleston.

"What a fascinating man," Joy mused as they walked across East Battery Street toward the seawall. "I hope the historical society has taken his oral history."

"I do too." Evelyn led Joy up the seawall. Tourists and locals were walking along the sidewalk, gawking out at the harbor, running, or simply meandering.

"Do you believe any of the things Mr. Hawk said?" Joy asked.

"I believe that *he* believes them," Evelyn conceded. "But I don't believe there's any validity to the sightings."

"What do you think people are seeing then?"

"What their minds and hearts want them to see. True love is a powerful force, to be sure, and people want to believe that it transcends death. I think, for those reasons, people love stories like Queenie Bennett's. They want to know that even death can't stop true love from conquering all."

Joy sighed. "I'd love to think that Wilson is still able to communicate with me, even though he's passed on. Sometimes, I can feel his presence, in a way. But I don't think it's because his spirit is still here. I think it's more about the memories I hold so dear to my heart. They take up a physical space in my brain, and, in that way, he's still here with me."

Evelyn linked arms with Joy. She often forgot that Joy was widowed. Times like this must be harder for her than others.

Joy smiled and squeezed Evelyn's arm close.

"I'm so happy you decided to come to Charleston after you lost Wilson," Evelyn said. "My life is so much richer because of your friendship."

"I feel the same way."

Their work was done at Mercy for the day, and they lived close to the hospital, so they walked toward their homes.

"How are things going with Shelby?" Joy asked.

It was Evelyn's turn to sigh. "She spends a lot of time in her bedroom, on her phone. James and I have made several suggestions for fun things we can see and do while she's visiting, but she says no to everything."

"Have you talked with her dad about what kind of trouble she was in before she came to Charleston?"

"A little. She was skipping school, got caught smoking on the school grounds, and was failing her classes. He didn't go into any details about why she was suspended, but I wasn't surprised."

"But you believe her when she says she didn't take the coin?"

"I want to believe her." The truth was, Evelyn wasn't completely sure that Shelby was innocent.

"Maybe, if you find out what got her suspended, it could shed more light on the current situation."

"You mean, if she was caught stealing?"

Joy didn't say anything as she gave Evelyn an apologetic look.

"I wonder if she'd tell me the truth," Evelyn mused.

Twenty minutes later, Evelyn had her opportunity to ask Shelby.

The smell of onions, vegetables, and chicken filled Evelyn's nose as she entered the house. After setting her keys in the calling card dish, she peeked into the living room down the hall, looking for her niece.

Shelby didn't appear to be on the main level.

"Hello," James called from the kitchen.

"It smells good in here." Evelyn walked into the kitchen and found James wearing his grilling apron to prevent the inevitable splatter from the hot oil. He was making stir-fry for supper.

He had a big grin on his face. "You look pretty today."

She leaned over and kissed him. "Thank you. Surprisingly, I felt a little underdressed this afternoon when I had tea on the harbor."

"Tea on the harbor?"

She explained how she and Joy had met Mr. Hawk and told James a little about the family history. Then she asked, "Is Shelby in her room?"

"I think so." He poured a bowl of fresh broccoli into the wok. "I almost forget she's here most days. It's just as quiet as usual around here."

"Do you need help with supper, or do you mind if I go talk to her?"

"I think I have everything under control. Supper should be ready in about fifteen minutes." He tossed the broccoli. "Anything in particular you need to talk to her about? Did something come up today?"

"No." Evelyn couldn't hide her frustration. "There are no leads. It's as if the coin just vanished, like Hunter O'Reilly said, into thin air."

"Did the police dust for fingerprints at the museum?"

"Yes—but there were none on the coin display. Not even Adam's, and he was the last one to touch the case."

"But he would have been wearing cotton gloves, right?"

"I suppose so."

"Then whoever took the coin was probably wearing gloves too."

"That, or they cleaned up after themselves."

"Interesting." James continued to stir the broccoli. "So, whoever did it knew what they were doing."

"What do you mean?"

"They knew how to get into the museum, how to open the case, and how to clean up." He leaned closer and said quietly, "Does that sound like a teenager?"

"No—but Shelby was there all day, watching the curators working. She was asking a lot of questions too. It wouldn't have been hard for her to figure it out."

"Right. But what about that other museum lady you told me about? Dr. Langer. She would know how to get into the case, wouldn't she? And she'd know enough to wear cotton gloves like Adam while handling a rare artifact."

It was definitely something to think about. "But how did she get into the museum without being spotted by the camera?"

"You haven't spoken to her yet?"

"No. Maybe I should go and see her first thing on Monday morning."

"Probably isn't a bad idea, though she might not be happy to see you."

"I'm sure she won't be." Evelyn took one of the raw carrot pieces and snacked on it, thinking about how she'd find time to get to the Charleston Museum. "There's just so much for me to do at work." Even though it was Friday evening and James was making a nice meal, the cares of the week wouldn't leave Evelyn in peace. "Things are getting so backed up in Records, and with the delay from the police investigation, we'll have to work extra hard to have the museum ready in time for the grand opening. The last thing I need is to be taking time off work to chase down this coin."

"When you find it, it'll be worth it in the end."

"You're right." Evelyn sighed. "I'm going to run up and talk with Shelby."

"Let her know supper's almost ready."

Evelyn left the kitchen and went up the stairs. She took a left at the top and walked to Shelby's bedroom. As always, the door was closed.

"Shelby?" Evelyn knocked on the door, but if it was like all the other times, Shelby probably had earbuds in and couldn't hear her. "I'm coming in." Evelyn slowly opened the door.

Shelby was on her bed, her phone in front of her face, with her white earbuds in her ears. She looked up at Evelyn, a question in her eyes as she took out one of the earbuds. "Yeah?"

"Supper's almost ready."

"Okay." Shelby took out the other earbud and turned to put her feet on the ground.

Evelyn walked into the room a little farther. "Hey. Can I ask you something?"

"What?" Shelby was wearing her black eyeliner again, but her hair was still blond.

"I never did ask you why you got suspended from school." Evelyn leaned against the desk, trying to act nonchalant, though she felt conspicuous.

Shelby shrugged. "Whatever. It's not a big deal."

"Getting suspended from school with just a month left is kind of a big deal. It must have been pretty serious."

"It wasn't even my fault."

"Says everyone who's ever been suspended."

Shelby rolled her eyes, but a half smile tilted her lips.

"If it wasn't your fault," Evelyn said, "then who's to blame?"

"My boyfriend, Rodney."

"I didn't know you had a boyfriend."

"He's the reason Dad sent me to Charleston. He thinks Rodney is a bad influence."

"Is he?"

Again, the shrug.

"Yet"—Evelyn moved away from the desk and sat on the bed next to Shelby—"when I said we might send you back, you didn't want to go. Don't you want to be with Rodney?"

"I don't know. I'm kind of tired of him."

"What did he do to get you in trouble?"

Shelby sighed. "He broke into the principal's office and stole the petty cash."

Evelyn's eyes widened at the news. "How did that get *you* into trouble?"

Shelby looked down at her ripped jeans and pulled at the threads. "Rodney is twenty-one. He's not a student at the school. I helped him get in."

"Shelby." Evelyn couldn't hide the shock from her voice. "Why did you do something like that—and what are you doing with a twenty-one-year-old man?"

"You sound just like my dad."

"Because we're both worried about you. Rodney doesn't sound like a good guy—especially if he uses you to break into buildings."

Shelby grunted. "He's not a good guy. That's why I don't want to go back."

"Why did you do it?"

"I didn't know why he wanted to get into the principal's office. I thought he was gonna play a joke or cause a little trouble. It was exciting at the time. I didn't know he was going to steal."

Evelyn's heart beat a little faster as a thought occurred to her. "You didn't help Rodney get into the hospital museum, did you?"

"No!" Shelby stood and turned to Evelyn. "I told you, I didn't take the coin—and I don't know who did."

"Okay." Evelyn held up her hands. "I hear you."

"Whatever." Shelby rolled her eyes again and left the room. "I'm not going to tell you anything anymore," she said over her shoulder.

She stomped through the hall and down the stairs.

Evelyn just sat there on the bed, wondering if there was more to Shelby's story than she was letting on.

Chapter Eight

On Monday morning, Evelyn and Shirley walked up the concrete steps into the Charleston Museum. Evelyn's muscles were tight with apprehension, but she was thankful that Shirley had volunteered to come with her on her day off. It was a little less daunting to face Dr. Langer with a friend at her side.

"How was your weekend?" Shirley asked Evelyn, holding the door open for her to enter the museum.

Evelyn sighed. The weekend had not been relaxing or rejuvenating, with Shelby's constant attitude and her desire to stay home, in her bedroom, on her phone. "James and I suggested several fun outings to local museums and attractions, but Shelby didn't want to do anything. So we spent Saturday doing odd jobs around the house while Shelby sat on her bed."

On Sunday, Evelyn had insisted that Shelby join them for church, which she did—with an attitude—but as soon as they came home after enjoying lunch out, Shelby returned to her favorite perch.

"It's a new week," Shirley said with a smile in her voice. "Maybe things will start to improve."

"Between Shelby's unhappiness and the missing coin, I feel like everything is spinning out of control." Evelyn shook her head. "At least by confronting Dr. Langer I feel like I'm *doing* something, even if I don't discover anything helpful today."

"You never know." Shirley shrugged, her positive mood brightening Evelyn's.

The Charleston Museum was a large, boxy building, with little character or architectural significance. Brown brick dominated the outside structure, while echoing halls and high ceilings dwarfed the occupants within. The main lobby was a cold space, with an open stairway leading to exhibits on the second floor. It was evident that the curators took great pride in their work, and it showed. The organization was one of the oldest in the country and represented more than just the city of Charleston. There were exhibits highlighting the entire Low Country of South Carolina, including the medical exhibit that had once housed Blackbeard's medicine chest.

Evelyn had been to the museum on a few different occasions as a visitor but had never been there to see Dr. Langer. After asking at the round information desk, Evelyn and Shirley followed the directions to the director's office on the main level, tucked into the corner.

Dr. Langer was in her office, on the phone, when Evelyn tapped on her door. A long, narrow window beside the door allowed Evelyn to get a glimpse inside. The room was large but unremarkable. A bookshelf dominated one wall, a substantial desk sat in the middle, and a few potted plants stood by a window. It was neat and orderly, with a view looking into a courtyard, where a palm tree swayed in the breeze.

Shirley was quiet as she stood beside Evelyn.

The expression on Dr. Langer's face when she saw them might have been comical, if Evelyn had been in the mood to laugh. At first,

Dr. Langer looked surprised—but it was soon followed by irritation and disdain.

"Doesn't she like you?" Shirley asked.

"I get the distinct impression that she does not."

After what felt like ten minutes, Dr. Langer finally got off her phone and stood to open the door. She appeared to be in no hurry to address Evelyn and Shirley's presence.

"What are you doing here?" Dr. Langer asked, her greeting just as cool as the museum building. Her curly red hair was in disarray, as if dealing with it was an afterthought.

"Hello, Dr. Langer," Evelyn said. "This is my friend, Shirley Bashore. May we come in and speak to you?"

"What is this about? I have a busy schedule today."

"I'm sorry for interrupting you. Would you like us to make an appointment and come back later?"

"You're here now." Dr. Langer shook her head in exasperation and opened the door wider. "You might as well come in."

Evelyn and Shirley entered her office, taking chairs opposite from Dr. Langer with the desk in between. The chair was uncomfortable, but Evelyn wouldn't complain. She just wanted to get this meeting over with.

"What are you doing here, Mrs. Perry?" Dr. Langer asked. "I've returned all the items you recalled. I don't believe I have anything else you'd like—unless you want to start taking items that belong to us."

"I'm not here to take anything." Evelyn repositioned herself on the chair, setting her purse in her lap. "I've come to ask you about Lieutenant Dixon's coin."

"You mean, the coin you lost?"

"I didn't lose the coin. It was stolen."

"In the fifteen years I've worked in this museum—this huge, heavily visited museum—we've never had anything stolen. Yet here you are, with a tiny, insignificant museum, with no visitors, and you've lost one of the most intriguing finds of the twentieth century." She straightened a stack of papers on her desk, her lips tilting up in satisfaction. "I hate to tell you I told you so—but it seems appropriate, don't you think?"

Evelyn forced herself to remain calm as she shared a look with Shirley. "I haven't come here to argue with you—"

"Why have you come?"

It took all of Evelyn's willpower not to retaliate with the same attitude Dr. Langer was exhibiting. Instead, she took a slow, steady breath and said, "I've come to ask you about the coin."

"What could I possibly tell you? It's rare and a shame that you lost it."

"We didn't lose it," Shirley spoke up, as if to remind Dr. Langer. "It was stolen."

"Under your watch," Dr. Langer said.

Evelyn pressed her hands together, trying to keep calm. "I'm wondering where you were the night it was stolen."

Dr. Langer stared at Evelyn, her face filling with incredulity. "Are you *serious*?"

"You were one of the last people to see the coin," Evelyn said. "And your threat to the hospital museum would lend itself to a motive."

"You have got to be kidding me." Dr. Langer stood, her hands on the desk, and scowled at Evelyn. Color rose up her neck and into her cheeks, turning her freckled skin splotchy. "In all my life, I have never been more insulted. I am a professional museum director. It is my job to protect and maintain public history for future generations to enjoy. I take that responsibility very seriously. To think that I could do something so heinous as steal an artifact is incomprehensible."

Though Evelyn wanted to shy away from this conversation, there was too much at stake. Not only her career and reputation but her future. If she didn't find the coin, and the conservation center decided to press charges, Evelyn could be facing a long battle. The very thought sent a shiver up her back and made her press on. "I'm not accusing you, Dr. Langer." She stood to be eye level with the other woman. "I'm simply asking where you were that night. If you have nothing to hide, then you should have no reason to refuse answering."

"I will not deign to reply." Dr. Langer walked to her door and opened it. "You had no business starting a museum with the precious artifacts in your possession. That is a fact—one I have made clear—but it is no reason to *steal* something. Anyone could see that you were in over your head." She took a deep breath and lifted her chin. "It's time for both of you to leave. This conversation is over."

Shirley rose from her chair as Evelyn gripped her purse. She walked to the door but stopped to say, "If you won't give me an alibi for the night the coin went missing, I'll be forced to share your hostile attitude toward our museum with the police."

"By all means. I'd be happy to talk to them about the poor security you had in place at your museum. I'm sure everyone would like to know that your incompetence led to this travesty."

Evelyn held her head high as she walked out of Dr. Langer's office, Shirley close behind.

Several staff members looked their way, no doubt having heard part of their exchange. But Evelyn didn't care.

"Did you notice how defensive she was?" Shirley asked. "And she didn't give you a straight answer."

Evelyn nodded. Dr. Langer was an angry woman and, in Evelyn's opinion, she was capable of taking the coin. She was still high on Evelyn's suspect list.

It was almost a mile and a half from Mercy Hospital to the Charleston Museum, so Shirley had given Evelyn a ride. Evelyn had called Stacia and Adam to tell them she'd be late that morning, and after her encounter with Sarah Langer, she was thankful for a bit of time to cool off and air her frustration with Shirley.

The morning was already proving to be hot, but the sun was hidden behind a bank of clouds and the humidity was low. Evelyn took in several calming, deep breaths as she got into Shirley's car.

"Do you think Dr. Langer is responsible for the coin's disappearance?" Shirley asked as she pulled onto Meeting Street.

"If so, how?" Evelyn asked. "Did she somehow manipulate the security footage? Seamus seems to have a good handle on his surveillance system. I doubt she could have messed with it."

"Maybe she did it a different way. A way we haven't considered." Shirley turned down the air-conditioning. "All I know is that she doesn't seem to like us very much."

"It's not you, it's me. Our first interaction was after I requested the return of Blackbeard's medicine chest, and she hasn't liked me ever since. I don't usually have a problem with people, but when it comes to Dr. Langer, we can't see eye to eye."

"Maybe it's her superior attitude or her lack of confidence in your abilities." Shirley offered a sympathetic smile. "This might not even be about you—I'm sure this has to do with her disappointment over the artifact."

"You're probably right. I shouldn't take her anger personally." Evelyn put her face in her palm as she looked out the window. "But if it wasn't Dr. Langer who took the coin, then was it Shelby? Maybe she found a way into the museum—or worse, maybe her boyfriend came to town and talked her into letting him into the museum. She was gone that night and won't tell me where she went."

"Have you talked to her dad about all this?"

"Some of it, but I've been so busy. I should probably call him." Evelyn pulled her cell phone out of her purse. "Do you mind if I try him now? I might not get another chance today."

"Go ahead."

It had been a week since Eric dropped Shelby off in Charleston. Other than a couple of texts between them, they hadn't spoken.

Evelyn touched a few icons and found Eric's number. He was almost eight years younger than Evelyn and had been more of a responsibility than a playmate when they were children. They'd never been particularly close, and when their parents purchased the house Evelyn now owned, their marriage had been rocky for several years. That added to the chaos and tension in the house, and Evelyn tried to be away from home as much as possible. Then she went off to college when he was ten years old, and soon after, married James. She had hoped that taking care of Shelby would help bridge the gap in their relationship, but that would only happen if she reached out to him.

Shirley stopped at a red light as the phone rang in Evelyn's ear.

"Hello?" Eric said.

"Hi." Evelyn sat up straighter. "Is this a good time to talk?"

"Not really. I'm at work. Is something wrong?"

Evelyn took a moment to steady her thoughts. "Actually, there is something. I've been trying to avoid calling you, but I think you should know."

"What did she do now?"

"That's the thing, I don't know if she did it."

"What happened?"

Evelyn quickly explained the situation with the coin.

Eric didn't speak until Evelyn came to the end of her story. "And she denies it?"

"Yes. I want to believe she's innocent, but she doesn't have any witnesses to prove that she wasn't at the hospital that night."

"Has she been in contact with Rodney?"

"I don't know. She told me about him—about why she was suspended from school. Do you think he could have come here?"

"I would be surprised if he didn't end up there at some point."

"Why didn't you tell me about that possibility when you brought her?" Evelyn frowned. "That's pretty important information, and I could've been better prepared."

"I was upset," he said. "Shelby and I fought the whole drive to your house. I wasn't thinking about all the possibilities at the time."

"At least Shelby sounds like she's not interested in seeing him again."

"Yeah, she says that a lot. I wouldn't put it past her to lie for him—she's done it before." Eric let out a frustrated groan. "I'm sorry I got you mixed up in this, Evie."

Evelyn sighed. "There's not a lot we can do about it now. I wanted to let you know what's happening and ask a little bit more about Shelby. She doesn't talk much."

"Do you want me to come and get her?" He didn't sound excited about the idea.

Shirley turned her car left onto Broad Street. She didn't appear as if she was listening to the conversation, but how could she not?

"No. She's fine here," Evelyn said. "I want her to stay. I just wish I knew how to crack her shell."

"If you figure it out, would you tell me?" He sounded exhausted again, and Evelyn thought about how tired she was after only a week with her teenage niece. She couldn't imagine how parents dealt with rebellion day in and day out without time off.

"Shelby told me she helped Rodney break into the school—but what other things should I know?"

"It wasn't just the school." He paused for a second. "She also stole from me. She took my credit card and ran up some serious debt. Mostly things for Rodney to sell. That kid is trouble. I hope and pray he stays away from her. He was the main reason I wanted to get her out of here."

"Again," Evelyn said in frustration, "this was information you should have shared with me. I knew about a few of her mistakes, but I didn't realize she was using your credit card."

"I didn't think it mattered, since she was doing it for him. I was hoping that if I got her away from him, she'd stop breaking the law. She didn't do any of this before he was around."

"Does Rodney live in Jacksonville?"

"Unfortunately, yes."

"What's his last name?"

"Fletcher."

"Did you press charges?"

"No—but I should have. He spent some time in jail after stealing the petty cash, but the school decided not to press charges against Shelby, because she was only seventeen. She got suspended, and I decided to send her to California."

"And that's still the plan?"

"As far as I know. I haven't spoken to Wanda in a couple of weeks."

"I hope, for Shelby's sake, that moving to California is the best thing for her."

"So do I. If it wasn't for Rodney, I wouldn't be encouraging her to go. But she needs some distance from him."

Shirley turned onto Tradd Street and the hospital came into view.

Evelyn was almost afraid to ask the next question. "Any other trouble I should know about?"

"I've caught her in several lies—all of them connected to Rodney. But I know, in her heart, she's a good kid. She just needs a fresh start."

"She is a good kid, Eric. She's just hurting."

"I don't want her to do anything she'll regret later on. It's one thing to be hurting and struggling to put yourself together. It's another thing to make choices that will haunt you for the rest of your life."

Evelyn longed to reassure her brother but didn't know what to say.

Shirley pulled into the main entrance and stopped the car, smiling at Evelyn to let her know she didn't need to hurry.

"I feel responsible," Eric said to Evelyn. "If I had been a better husband, Wand—"

"I'm sure you could have made different decisions along the way, but ultimately, she made the call to leave."

"Yeah." His response was lackluster. "Keep me informed about Shelby," he said. "If she gets to be too much to handle, I'll come and get her."

"She's doing fine right now."

"If Rodney shows up, don't hesitate to call the police."

"Okay. I love you, Eric."

"Love you too, Evie. And thanks. For everything."

"You're welcome. Bye." She hung up the phone and looked at Shirley. "Sorry you had to hear all that."

"It's okay, Evelyn. Families are messy. You sound like you're doing a great job with your brother—and with Shelby. This'll work itself out."

"I hope you're right." More now than ever, Evelyn wished Shelby had a better alibi for the night she was missing. If Evelyn could find someone who could vouch for her, then she could put her doubts and uncertainties to rest. "Thanks for coming with me to the museum."

"You're welcome. Let me know if you need anything else."

Evelyn got out of Shirley's car and walked into Mercy. She needed to do a little research on Rodney, but how? How could she find out if he was in Jacksonville that night, or if he had come to Charleston?

She was still pondering this when she entered the records department and found Stacia at her desk.

"Hey," Evelyn said to Stacia. "If I wanted to find out where someone was on a certain night, do you think I could do it through social media?"

"It's possible—if they have a public account and shared where they were that night."

"Could you do me a huge favor? Could you try to find a guy named Rodney Fletcher? He's twenty-one and lives in Jacksonville, Florida. That's all I know about him."

Stacia gave Evelyn a strange look but said, "Okay. I'll see what I can find."

"Thanks."

Evelyn wasn't sure if they would learn anything helpful, but she couldn't let this go. Shelby was keeping something from her, and Evelyn was afraid it was tied to Rodney.

"I'm heading over to open the museum for Adam."

"Tell him I said hi." Stacia smiled, a teasing gleam in her eyes.

"I will, but I don't know if he'll do anything about it."

Stacia's laughter followed Evelyn out the door.

Chapter Nine

EVELYN WAS BUSIER THAN EVER that day. And later, when she went home, Shelby complained of a migraine and stayed in her room during supper. When Evelyn checked on her before bed, Shelby was fast asleep, her mouth hanging open as she snored.

The next morning, when Evelyn checked on her again, she was still sleeping hard. Evelyn left her a note by her bed, telling her to call or text if she needed anything or if the headache was still bothering her.

Since she had arrived at work late the day before, Evelyn went to Mercy early that morning. It would be good to get a few things done before the workday began and the others showed up.

Stopping for her morning cup of coffee in the gift shop, Evelyn was surprised to find Anne and Shirley standing near the counter, talking quietly with Joy.

"Evelyn," Anne said, "I'm so happy you're here. We were just going to call you."

"Call me?" Evelyn lifted her eyebrows in surprise. "Why?"

Shirley was wearing a pair of pink scrubs, her cross necklace shining under the track lighting in the gift shop. "There was another sighting of Queenie last night. This one was caught on video too—near Mercy."

"Here?"

Joy nodded and turned her phone around so Evelyn could watch. "The person who posted this said it was about one in the morning, and he was walking by Mercy when he heard someone—or something—calling out in a low, mournful tone. When he saw who was making the noise—a figure in an old gown—he remembered the video from last week and started recording it."

The playback began, but it was so dark, it was hard to tell what Evelyn was watching. A man's voice could be heard, panting and whispering, as he said, "I just saw her, walking along the harbor, coming toward Mercy Hospital."

"Where is he?" Evelyn asked. "None of this looks familiar."

"Just watch," Anne said. "You'll see."

The video was bouncing as the man walked quickly. Soon he was in the Grove—passing the very table where Evelyn and her friends had eaten lunch a couple of days ago.

"There!" the man said in a whispered voice. "By the angel statue."

He stopped moving and the camera steadied—and that was when Evelyn saw the woman. She was too far away and it was too dark to make out her features, but she wore a long gown, her dark hair flowing down her back.

The woman didn't seem to notice the man recording her as she cried out for George. She moved past the statue and disappeared around the corner of a building.

"Was that her?" the man asked, his voice excited and high-pitched. "Did I just see a ghost?"

He followed after her, breathing heavier now than before. The camera caught another glimpse of her, and then she disappeared around another corner of the hospital, near the Angel Wing. She could be heard calling out for George, over and over. The cameraman started to run, but when he came to the corner, she was gone.

"Where did she go?" the guy asked, turning in a circle. "It's a dead end."

And, sure enough, it was. Two sides of the space were four-story walls of the Angel Wing, and the third side was made up of a tall fence that someone would need a ladder to climb over.

"She vanished," the voice said again. "I can't believe I just saw her." And then the video ended.

Evelyn didn't say a word as Joy pulled her phone back. She stared, trying to make sense of what she just saw.

"What do you think?" Anne asked Evelyn.

"Who was the cameraman?"

"The video was posted by a YouTube user named Charleston2022." Shirley shrugged. "It's his only video. He probably made the account just to post this clip."

"Did Mr. Hawk comment on this one too?" Evelyn looked to Joy.

Joy shook her head. "Not yet. It's still early, though."

"This looks just like the last woman," Shirley said. "If Mr. Hawk validated that sighting, he'll probably validate this one too."

"But who is this woman?" Evelyn asked. "We know it's not Queenie's ghost. But how does she keep disappearing like that? And why is she doing this?"

"Who knows?" Anne asked. "I've seen stranger things."

Evelyn nibbled her bottom lip. "I have a feeling we won't know unless we talk to her ourselves."

"What do you have in mind?" Shirley asked.

"A stakeout." Evelyn couldn't help but smile at the very idea.

"A stakeout?" Joy put her hand up to the lapel of her violet-colored blouse. "As in, dress in black and sit on the harbor all night, hoping and praying she'll decide to show up again?"

"That's exactly what I'm thinking." Evelyn's mind was turning with all sorts of ideas. "There's no other way we can possibly figure out her identity. And what if she's connected to the coin disappearance?"

"But what if she doesn't show up tonight?" Shirley asked. "This video was taken at one o'clock. How long do we wait—and how often do we go back? I need my sleep if I'm going to work the next day."

"I think it's a chance I need to take," Evelyn said. "If this woman knows anything about the missing coin, then I need to talk to her. Cyril Lorenzo is calling me every day, wondering if I've heard anything about the coin. I wouldn't be surprised if he starts pointing his finger at me—or Shelby."

Joy pressed her lips together and then said, "I'm in. I'll go on a stakeout with you."

Evelyn laid her hand on Joy's arm. "Thank you."

"Oh, why not?" Shirley said. "I can handle a sleepless night or two. I'm a nurse, after all."

"Well," Anne said, "if the three of you are going on a stakeout, then I want in too. I'm sure Ralph will be worried about me, but I think with the four of us together, we'll be pretty safe."

"We can find a place to park my car with a good view of the harbor and Mercy Hospital," Evelyn said. "How about we meet at eleven thirty tonight? Here at the hospital."

"I'll bring potato chips," Joy said. "And a thermos of coffee."

"I'll bring some homemade cookies." Anne's eyes lit up. "I'll make extra for Ralph to sweeten him up to this idea."

"And I'll bring some of my mama's cold fried chicken." Shirley grinned. "We'll need a little protein to keep up our strength."

Evelyn smiled at their enthusiasm, hoping that they would see the woman behind these sightings. Surely she had a reason for what she was doing.

After filling her mug with Joy's coffee, Evelyn went to the records department and began her work. Soon Stacia entered wearing a cute navy-blue romper with a jean jacket and a pair of white boat shoes. Her blond hair was caught up in a messy ponytail that looked like she'd taken her time to perfect. When she saw Evelyn, she smiled and her blue eyes lit up.

"Good morning," she said as she set her purse and water bottle on her desk. "I had some luck finding a man named Rodney Fletcher on Instagram." She pulled her phone out of her jacket pocket and turned it on. "Here." She showed the Instagram account to Evelyn. "If you scroll down, you'll see pictures of him and Shelby together."

Evelyn wrinkled her nose. Rodney was definitely older than Shelby—maybe even older than twenty-one. He had black hair and a thin black mustache.

"I wonder why Shelby wants to date someone so much older than she is," Evelyn said. "Aren't there seventeen-year-olds in Jacksonville she could date?"

Stacia shrugged, her voice teasing. "Maybe he's a good listener."

Evelyn wanted to roll her eyes, but she refrained. "Did he post anything the night the coin went missing?"

"Nope." Stacia pulled her phone back and looked at the screen again. "Nothing I could find, anyway. His last post was a night before the theft, and it looks like he was in Jacksonville at the time."

"Okay. Thanks for checking."

Stacia returned to her desk and then turned around. "Did you ever talk to the custodial staff? Maybe they saw something the night the coin was taken."

"That's a good idea." Evelyn stood. "I have to go open the museum for Adam and his team. Maybe I'll run downstairs to talk to the custodians after that. Thanks for thinking of it."

"You're welcome. I hope they know something helpful."

"Me too."

The custodial department of Mercy Hospital was housed in the basement of the Angel Wing, though they had several stations throughout the building and in each wing. The hospital employed an army of daytime and nighttime custodians, and, for the most part, they did their jobs efficiently and quietly—rarely getting the proper recognition, in Evelyn's opinion.

Over the years, the basement had been updated and remodeled, but it was still a dingy and musty space. Evelyn had never liked going into the lowest level of the hospital and was thankful she didn't have to do it often.

At the head of the department was Earl Sheffield, a man who had worked at Mercy for as long as Evelyn had been there, and maybe even longer. He had more energy than most people on staff, and he was never cranky or cross. On the contrary, he was a jolly man who was friends with everyone he met, and he never forgot a name. But what made him even more endearing was his crop of white hair and thick white beard. He kept it growing all year so he could play Santa Claus for the hospital staff party and for the children who were patients around the holidays.

When Evelyn tapped on his office door, he opened it with a wide grin. "Hello, Evelyn. What brings you down into my lair today?"

He teased everyone about his basement office, but he didn't truly seem to mind. He had generous windows, though they were up near the ceiling. They let in a ton of natural light, even if all a person could see was the trees and sky beyond.

"Hi, Earl. Do you have a minute to chat?" Evelyn asked.

"Always." He opened his door wider. There were three other desks in his office, two of which were occupied by custodial supervisors who worked under Earl to manage the huge complex of buildings at Mercy. "You remember Oscar Maverick and Dale Olson?"

Evelyn smiled at the two men. Oscar was middle-aged, with a narrow face and graying whiskers. Since he was the supervisor in charge of the Angel Wing, Evelyn saw him often. When she did, he was usually wearing a blue custodial shirt and a pair of jeans, like now. Dale was tall and broad, with dark skin and a short haircut. He was much younger and newer to Mercy. Evelyn wasn't sure which wing he supervised. "It's nice to see you both again."

"Do we need to speak in private?" Earl asked.

"No—I'd actually appreciate the chance to speak to all of you, if I could."

"Of course. Pull up a chair." Earl moved a stack of folders off a chair and indicated that Evelyn should take a seat.

The room was cool—a nice byproduct of being in the basement. Evelyn sat forward in the chair, eagerly searching each man's face as she told them why she had come.

"I'm sure you've all heard about the missing coin from our new museum."

All three men nodded.

"It didn't occur to me until today that one of you or your staff might have noticed something suspicious in the museum. The police searched the space but could find no clues. It's almost as if the coin just disappeared."

Images of Queenie filled Evelyn's mind as she thought about how the woman had vanished on both videos they had watched. But she pushed them aside to give her full attention to these men.

Earl pressed his lips together, his white whiskers moving as he shook his head. "I'm sorry, but I haven't heard anything strange or unusual from any of my staff. I did hear about the coin—but I don't think any of our people were even in the museum around the time it disappeared."

Evelyn looked to Oscar and Dale, but they shook their heads in unison.

"What about before the coin was taken?" Evelyn asked. "Any time your staff was in that room? Did they see anything strange then? You were in there a couple of days before we received the coin to dust and do a cleanup in preparation for the artifact installation, right? I'm wondering if anyone heard or saw something."

Earl shook his head again, but he looked to Oscar. "You supervise the Angel Wing. Have any of your team members noticed anything or said anything out of the usual?"

Oscar's face was without emotion as he shook his head, looking from Earl to Evelyn. He dropped his gaze to his desk and picked up a paperclip and absently played with it. "I can't say that I've heard or seen anything, and no one's said a word about the museum. If you don't count the complaining."

"Complaining?" Evelyn asked, frowning.

"About the extra work it'll be now that the museum is coming together. It'll add a couple extra hours onto our workload to go in there every night and wipe down the exhibits, vacuum, and the like. No one consulted us when y'all decided to start a museum."

Evelyn hadn't even considered the custodial staff and what it meant for them. "I'm sorry. You're right. We should have consulted you. Is there anything I can do to alleviate your concerns?"

He snorted. "It's a little too late for that, don't you think?"

"Uh." Earl cleared his throat and frowned at Oscar. "That's a matter we'll take up internally here in our department. Evelyn doesn't need to be worrying about our workload. She's got enough on her plate as it is."

Evelyn appreciated Earl's attitude, but she tried to smile at Oscar to let him know she was truly sorry.

He ignored her and continued to play with the paperclip.

"If none of you have heard anything that might be helpful," Evelyn said as she stood to take her leave, "I should probably get back to Records and let you get back to your work. Please contact me if something comes up."

Earl also stood, smiling. "Of course. I'll be sure to speak to each of our team members personally and ask if they've seen or heard anything of interest."

"I appreciate that, Earl. Thank you." She smiled at Dale and Oscar again, and then she went to the exit.

As she turned to close the door, she saw Oscar watching her, his scowl still firmly in place.

She had no idea she'd caused such a stir in the custodial department with the addition of her museum.

Could Oscar's anger be enough motivation to cause trouble?

Chapter Ten

It was eleven that evening when Evelyn started to gather her things to leave the house and meet her friends at Mercy for their stakeout.

"Are you sure this is a good idea?" James asked as he came into the kitchen, where Evelyn was filling a cooler with water bottles.

"What could go wrong? It's just a woman playing make-believe."

"Not everything is as it seems, Evie. What if this woman is delusional? What if she's dangerous?"

"She hasn't caused any trouble."

"Yet."

Evelyn closed the small cooler and lifted her purse over her shoulder. "We're going to watch from the car. If it looks dangerous, I won't approach her." She frowned. "What I'm more concerned about is Shelby. Did she even leave her room today?"

"Not while I was home." James leaned against the counter and crossed his arms. "Do you think we should take her to the doctor?"

"I don't know. She won't talk to me about her headache." Shelby was still complaining of a migraine and hadn't come downstairs in two days. Evelyn and James had taken food and beverages up to her room, but there wasn't much else they could do. "I don't know if she suffers from these often or if this is the first one. Does she need special medicine, or will the ibuprofen I brought to her be enough? She just wants to sleep."

"Do you think she's depressed?" James's brow furrowed in concern.

"I think she's struggling with some form of depression—but is she under a doctor's care or is she just trying to get through this on her own?" Evelyn let out a weary breath. "I feel like I'm walking in the dark where she's concerned. If she's not willing to communicate with me, then I don't know how to help her."

"Maybe you should call Eric again," James suggested. "See if he has any insight into her physical and mental health."

"That's a good idea. I texted him about this, but he hasn't responded. If she's not feeling better by tomorrow morning, I'll call him and have a chat with him."

"In the meantime"—James smiled and shook his head—"you be careful out there."

"I will." Evelyn smiled back and gave him a kiss. "Call me if you need me."

James gave her a hug, and then Evelyn left the house through the back door. She put her cooler and bag in the back seat, pulled out of their driveway, and headed toward Mercy Hospital.

The women had agreed to meet at the main entrance at eleven thirty, so when Evelyn pulled up ten minutes early, she was a little surprised to see Anne, Shirley, and Joy all standing there waiting.

"Is everyone excited?" Evelyn asked her friends as she got out of the car.

"Nervous might be a better word to describe how I'm feeling," Anne admitted as she opened one of the back doors. "Ralph thinks we're looking for trouble."

"I'm not looking for trouble," Evelyn said. "I'm looking for answers."

Shirley, who had her hand in her oversized bag, said, "And I'm looking for my peanut M&Ms."

Everyone laughed as they got into the car. Joy sat up in front with Evelyn, and Shirley joined Anne in the back.

"Where do you think we should park and wait?" Joy asked as Evelyn pulled out of the main entrance and took a left onto East Bay Street.

"We should probably park somewhere between the two locations where she was spotted," Shirley said from the back seat.

Joy opened a bottle of sparkling water. "That would be close to Mr. Hawk's house."

"That's as good a place as any." Evelyn didn't have far to drive. Soon they were parked with a good view of the harbor and Mercy Hospital, which loomed above the seashore. Most of the lights were on in each wing, though a few of the patient rooms were dark.

"Did everyone use the bathroom before we left?" Anne asked.

"Yes, Mom," Shirley responded in a teasing manner.

Joy took a sip of her water. "So, what's our plan? If this person *did* take the coin, then what else might she be willing to do? Are we really going to approach her?"

"If we see her," Evelyn said, "I'll go talk to her. I have to."

"Aren't you a little nervous?" Anne asked Evelyn.

"I'm nervous about the coin, but I'm hoping and trusting that God has His hand in this matter. The guilty party is out there somewhere, and if it's God's will, I believe we'll eventually catch him or her."

"And until then," Joy said, "we'll keep searching for answers."

Everyone was quiet for a minute, and then Anne said, "We might as well get the snacks out. This could be a long wait. I made three different kinds of cookies."

"This doesn't seem so bad, does it?" Evelyn mused as she looked around the street. There were a few lights to illuminate the road and sidewalks. The seawall was dark, but there were still a few people walking along the top. It was a safe part of historic Charleston, and they were inside their car with the doors locked.

"Not with all our food." Anne laughed as she opened the large bag she'd brought from home. She took out three containers. "I have chocolate chip, oatmeal raisin, and macadamia nut."

"This isn't bad at all," Shirley agreed as she reached for a cookie.

As the time slipped by, the four friends laughed and talked while keeping an eye on their surroundings. Eventually, the street turned quiet and emptied of all pedestrians. A vehicle drove by on occasion, but all the houses in the area were dark and very little moved.

Evelyn had partially opened the windows to allow in a breeze. The sound of the ocean waves beating against the wall began to lull her senses. She felt sleepy around midnight, though the conversation had been stimulating.

"How long are we going to wait?" Shirley asked on a yawn.

"The two sightings were between midnight and a little after one, right?" Evelyn asked.

"That's what I understand," Joy said.

"Then I say we wait until one thirty. If we don't see anything before that, we go home."

"Sounds good to me," Anne said.

Another twenty minutes passed, the conversation started to wane, and Evelyn's eyes were getting heavy. She was just about to suggest they call it a night when she caught movement in the driver's sideview mirror. Someone was standing close to the seawall. It was hard to make out who it might be with the darkness and shadows, but it looked like a woman.

"I think I see someone," Evelyn said quietly to her friends.

All three of them became alert at Evelyn's comment.

"Where?" Anne asked, looking all around.

"Behind us—near the seawall. It looks like a woman, but she's not moving. At least, she's not moving much. I just barely noticed her. I don't know how long she's been there."

Shirley turned to look out the back window. "Where? It's so dark, how did you see?"

The figure moved again, but she didn't leave her spot near the wall.

"Oh—I see. I think it *is* a woman."

"What is she doing?" Anne asked. "Why is she just standing there?"

No one answered Anne as they continued to watch.

The figure stood there for several more minutes without moving.

"Do you think she's homeless?" Anne asked. "Maybe she's just camping out there for the night."

"She's standing," Joy said. "If she was camping out there, don't you think she'd be lying on the ground?"

"Can you tell if she's wearing a gown?" Evelyn asked. "Does it look like the woman who's been portraying Queenie?"

"I can't tell," Shirley said.

A few more minutes passed, and Evelyn said, "I'm going to step out and get a better look."

"She could be dangerous," Anne warned. "Why don't we just wait a little longer?"

"Because I'm tired, and I want to know who she is." Evelyn turned off her dome lights so they wouldn't light up as she opened her car door. "Anyone coming with me?"

"I'll come." Shirley moved her things around in the back, setting her bag on the seat next to her.

"I think I'll stay here," Joy said, "and keep on the lookout for anyone else."

"I'll stay with Joy," Anne offered.

"Ready?" Evelyn asked Shirley.

"Yes, ma'am." Shirley opened her door at the same moment as Evelyn.

They stepped out of the car and closed their doors quietly.

Despite Evelyn's claim to not be nervous, her heart was pumping hard and her palms had begun to sweat. Were they about to approach the woman who was pretending to be Queenie? Or was this woman just an innocent bystander?

Evelyn and Shirley walked along the seawall, both of them wearing dark clothing.

The wind had picked up, gusting off the ocean and tossing Evelyn's hair.

She knew the moment the woman spotted them, because the dark figure stood straighter and started to walk away.

"Wait!" Evelyn called.

The woman was wearing a long skirt, her hair flowing down her back like the one in the video. Was this the woman they were waiting for?

It didn't take long for Evelyn and Shirley to catch up to her.

"Wait!" Evelyn said again. "We just want to ask you a question."

The woman slowed and turned. "Evelyn?"

Evelyn and Shirley paused. It was still too dark to know who the woman was—but she obviously recognized Evelyn's voice.

"Who are you?" Evelyn asked.

"It's me, Jerica Dixon."

A sinking feeling hit the bottom of Evelyn's gut. "Jerica? What are you doing out here?" Was she the one pretending to be Queenie?

"I'm here to catch the imposter."

"What imposter?" Shirley asked.

"The one people think is Queenie Bennett. I think she's the one who took the coin."

Evelyn and Shirley were now standing in front of Jerica. She had her arms crossed as she addressed them.

"Why do you think she's guilty?" Evelyn asked, still not convinced that Jerica wasn't the one impersonating Queenie.

"It's too coincidental," Jerica said. "The coin goes missing and then this person starts to make appearances. There's got to be a connection."

Shirley glanced from Evelyn to Jerica. "Have you been here long?"

"This is my second night. I plan to stay until dawn, if I have to. When I catch her, I'll make a citizen's arrest and take her to the police." Jerica nodded once, as if her mind was made up.

"I don't think you can make a citizen's arrest unless you have proof."

"Hmm." Jerica looked to the side. "I hadn't thought of that." Then she glanced back at Evelyn. "What are *you* doing here?"

"Waiting for Queenie to appear," Evelyn said. "But I'm only planning to question her."

"It probably doesn't pay for all of us to be here," Shirley said to Jerica. "You can go home if you'd like. We'll tell you if we find her."

"Yeah, right!" Jerica shook her head. "And miss all the action? No, thanks. I'm staying right here until I catch this pretender. Or—or, can I join you?"

Evelyn shrugged as she looked to Shirley. Maybe another pair of eyes would be helpful. It couldn't hurt.

When Evelyn opened her door and Anne and Joy saw Jerica, their faces revealed their surprise.

"Hi," Jerica said to them, bending down to look into the back seat. "Remember me?"

"We'll need to keep our voices down," Evelyn said quietly to Jerica. "Or we might scare away anyone who's out here."

"Oh, right. My bad." Jerica put her finger up to her lips. "Mum's the word."

Anne and Joy looked at Evelyn with questions in their gazes.

"Jerica asked if she could join us," Evelyn explained.

"It's not very fun—and kind of creepy—to be out here by yourself," Jerica said. "Mind if I squeeze into the back seat with you?"

"I don't think we'll need to worry about squeezing in," Joy said as she pointed toward Mercy Hospital. "Look."

A woman was walking slowly near the end of the seawall toward the hospital. She was wearing a long, full skirt, and her hair was unbound, blowing wildly behind her.

"It's her!" Jerica said on an excited whisper, grabbing Evelyn by the arm and jumping up and down. "It's really, really her."

"Shh," Evelyn said, reminding Jerica to be quiet. "We don't want her to hear us or she'll probably run."

Jerica quieted and nodded. "What do we do?"

"A couple of us need to follow her and try to get close to her before she realizes we're there, or she's going to disappear again."

"Okay—who's coming with me?" Jerica asked.

The last thing Evelyn wanted was for Jerica to be involved. The woman seemed easily excitable, and Evelyn was afraid Jerica would compromise her plan. They'd waited too long to lose Queenie now.

"How about we wait here?" Anne suggested to Jerica. "Shirley and Evelyn can go after her, since they know their way around Mercy Hospital so well."

Evelyn could have hugged Anne for her quick thinking.

Jerica moved her mouth back and forth like she was thinking about the logic—and then she said, "Okay. But I want in on the next adventure."

Queenie had already disappeared into the Mercy Hospital complex, which meant they might not spot her again.

"We'll be back as soon as we can," Evelyn said.

She and Shirley left the car and walked quickly up East Bay Street toward the hospital.

"I saw her turn into the Grove again," Shirley said. "She's probably heading back to where she was last night."

"I think I can hear her saying George's name." Evelyn listened intently as they drew closer and turned down the lane into the Grove.

It was dark, with only a few landscape lights to illuminate their path. The woman stood near the angel statue—and that was when Evelyn saw a man recording her. He was on the opposite side of the statue, his phone out in front.

"Good." he said. "This time, say George slower, like you did the first night."

"George," the woman said, letting her voice drag out the name in a low, lamenting tone.

Shirley and Evelyn stopped near one of the tables.

"They're in on it together," Evelyn whispered.

"Looks like it."

"Walk around the statue a few times," the man said. "I'll edit out whatever doesn't look right." He laughed with glee. "Our last video went viral—hopefully this one will too. We'll make millions with these videos, baby."

It was too hard to make out their features, so Evelyn motioned for Shirley to follow her. "We need to get a better look."

"Do you think they'll talk to us?"

"I doubt it, not if they're doing this to make money. But if we can identify them, maybe we can contact them a different way."

They snuck out from behind the table and quietly rushed over to the side of the building where there were no lights and it was shadowed.

"Hold up," the man said. "Someone's here. Go, go, go."

Evelyn had no time to wait. She and Shirley had been spotted. She rushed out of the shadows, trying to get a look at them.

The couple started to run.

Evelyn chased after them, Shirley at her side. Would the couple be dangerous? They didn't sound menacing—but who could know something like that?

It didn't take long before the two people disappeared around a corner and Evelyn lost them. She and Shirley were breathing hard, and Evelyn had to bend forward to catch her breath. Disappointment sliced through her. "We were so close! If they hadn't heard us, we might have found out who they were."

"I'm getting too old for this," Shirley said as she put her hands on her thighs and took a few deep breaths. "It's too dark and too late to be chasing people around dark corners."

"Let's head back and tell the others what happened."

"Lead the way."

They walked along the side of the hospital, and Evelyn kept her eyes and ears open, in case the couple showed up again. Moving around the angel statue, Evelyn looked up at her, recalling some of the stories she'd heard about it over the years. There were those who said the angel kept guard over the hospital, especially since the Angel Wing had survived the Charleston fire so long ago. Evelyn didn't believe any of it, but it was a nice thought. So many rumors and legends existed about the hospital, from the angel statue to the secret passageways.

Evelyn paused—her feet and her thoughts coming to a standstill.

"What?" Shirley asked.

"I have an idea." She motioned for Shirley to keep following her. "I'll tell you when we get back to the car."

Several minutes later, Evelyn and Shirley reached the vehicle and found Anne, Joy, and Jerica all waiting anxiously.

"Well?" Jerica asked. "What happened?"

"We saw her," Evelyn said. "And she had a guy recording her."

"But when they spotted us," Shirley said, "they ran off and we couldn't catch them."

"That's too bad," Jerica said. "I could have probably caught them."

Evelyn chose to ignore her comment. "On our way back, I thought about something I hadn't before. It's time I went into the museum and did a little more investigating. There has to be some way someone got in and out of the museum without being spotted."

"How do you think they did it?" Joy asked.

"I think they found a secret passage. Remember last year when we discovered the passageway that runs from outside the hospital into the Vault? Maybe there's another one."

"Why didn't we think of that?" Joy asked, shaking her head.

"I would go and look now," Evelyn continued, "but it's late, and we all need some sleep. We can look tomorrow."

"Do you really think you'll find another passageway?" Anne asked Evelyn.

"I do. It's the only explanation that makes sense."

Evelyn hoped and prayed she was right—and that maybe, finally, she had a lead.

Chapter Eleven

IT WAS ALMOST ONE IN the morning by the time Evelyn dropped her friends off at the main entrance to Mercy Hospital. Jerica's car had been parked on South Battery Street, near White Point Gardens Park, and she had gone back on her own.

"I'm sorry we didn't catch Queenie," Evelyn said as she stood outside her car to say goodbye and wait for the other three to gather their belongings.

"It's okay." Anne shrugged. "I'm just happy everyone is safe. I'm not terribly upset that you didn't have to confront them."

"Do you want us to meet you in the museum tomorrow to start looking for a passageway?" Shirley asked Evelyn as she slipped her bag over her shoulder.

"If you'd like to, I'd appreciate the help." Evelyn's eyes were heavy and all she wanted was to get home to bed, but they needed a plan. "I would like to get in there before Adam and his team. I don't want to be disruptive, and I'd like a little privacy as we look, but that means arriving well before eight."

"I'll be at work by six thirty," Joy said, covering a yawn.

"I can be here at seven," Shirley said. "My shift doesn't start until eight."

"Okay. I'll see you back here at seven then."

That was only six hours away—a daunting reality.

Evelyn looked to Anne.

"I'll see what I can do," Anne said, though she had the longest commute home. "It depends on how much sleep I can get tonight. My volunteer shift doesn't start until afternoon."

"Okay. Don't feel obligated to come."

"I won't." Anne gave Evelyn a quick hug. "Good night."

"Good night," Evelyn said. "Thanks for your help."

The friends waved goodbye, and Evelyn got into her car and pulled out of the entrance. It was a quick seven-minute drive home, for which Evelyn was especially thankful. When she arrived at the house, all the lights, except Shelby's, were turned off in the house.

Evelyn parked the car and used her key to get in through the back door. She was quiet as she clicked the lock and walked down the hall to set her things on the kitchen counter. Everything was so still and peaceful. Slowly, trying to avoid the squeaking steps, she walked up the stairs. Instead of going to her bedroom to get ready for bed, she decided to check on Shelby. She had slept so much these past two days, she was probably wide awake now—unless she was still suffering from her migraine.

Evelyn knocked on Shelby's door. "Mind if I come in?"

"Do I have a choice?"

"Ouch." Evelyn cringed. "I'm just checking in with you."

"Fine. Come in."

Evelyn opened the door and found Shelby lying on her rumpled bed in a pair of shorts and a T-shirt. Her face was devoid of makeup, and her hair was clean. She had her ever-present phone in her hands but glanced up at Evelyn with a raised eyebrow.

"Are you feeling better?" Evelyn asked.

"Yeah. The headache is finally gone."

"Do you get them often?"

Shelby shrugged. "Once in a while."

"Have you been to the doctor about them?"

"My dad took me a couple of months ago. They gave me some medicine, but I forgot it in Jacksonville."

Evelyn walked over to the bed and leaned against the footboard. "Maybe I can get the prescription sent to a pharmacy here in Charleston."

"What's the point? I'll be leaving in a couple of weeks."

"Well, it's an option if the headache comes back." Evelyn looked around the room. There were a few dirty clothes on the floor and a sweatshirt lying on the back of the desk chair. "You should run a load of laundry tomorrow while I'm at work. You didn't bring much with you, and most of it looks dirty."

Shelby didn't answer as she looked at her phone again.

Evelyn went to the closet. "There's a laundry basket in here." She put her hand on the knob—but Shelby jumped off the bed and stepped in front of her.

"What are you doing?" she asked.

Evelyn was so surprised, she took a step away from the closet. "I was going to get the laundry basket out for you."

Shelby rolled her eyes. "Don't worry about it. I can take care of my own dirty clothes. I'm not a baby."

It took Evelyn a moment to collect her thoughts. "I know you're not a baby. I just thought I could be helpful."

"Well, it's not helpful. I can get the basket out myself."

A horrible feeling came over Evelyn. "Are you hiding something in the closet, Shelby?"

"No." Shelby frowned and crossed her arms. "I just want you out of my space. I don't need a mom to take care of me. I've been fine for a year without one. I've got everything under control."

Evelyn returned Shelby's frown. *Was* she hiding something? And what would she do if Evelyn opened the closet to look? Was it within her right? Or did she need to leave well enough alone?

Could Shelby be hiding the coin in her closet?

The thought sent a chill down Evelyn's spine. "If you're hiding something in that closet, Shelby, I want to know what it is."

"I'm not hiding anything." Shelby stared at Evelyn, unflinching. "I just want you to leave me alone."

Evelyn studied her niece for another moment, wishing she could believe what she was saying. "If you are hiding something," she said again, "I'm trusting you to make the right choice. I won't force my way into that closet. But, Shelby, if it's the coin—"

"For the last time, I didn't take the coin!" Her words were angry and loud and full of hurt. Tears sprang to her eyes, and she threw herself down on the bed. "Can't you just leave me alone?"

Pain sliced through Evelyn's heart, but she nodded. She felt the need to apologize for accusing her again, but she also knew that it would fall on deaf ears right now.

"Good night." Evelyn slowly left Shelby's room and walked down the dark hallway to her own bedroom, her chest tight with emotions.

The moment she entered, James flipped on the bedside lamp and met Evelyn's gaze with bleary eyes. "What was all the shouting about?"

Evelyn was tired and weary. "I asked Shelby if she took the coin again, and she got angry with me."

He lay back on his pillow. "Do you want me to talk to her? She has no right to treat you that way."

"No." Evelyn slipped off her shoes, her feet aching. "I just want to go to bed. I need to get up in about five hours."

James was quiet for a moment while Evelyn began to change into her pajamas. "How did the stakeout go?" he asked.

"We saw Queenie again—and discovered that she and the cameraman are in cahoots, trying to make money with their videos."

"You talked to them?"

"No, but I overheard them. They disappeared when I chased them." She pulled the pencil out of her hair that she was using to keep it up in a twist. "I got an idea tonight though. Remember that hidden passageway we found last year, leading into the Vault? What if there's another one? What if it leads into the museum?"

James blinked several times as he seemed to consider her idea. "Who would know about another passageway?"

"It could be anyone. Tomorrow, I'm meeting Shirley and Evelyn and maybe Anne in the museum and we're going to look for it."

"Wow," was all James said.

"I'm tired." Evelyn pulled a T-shirt over her head. "Mind if I fill you in on the rest tomorrow?"

"Of course." He smiled. "Try to get some sleep."

Evelyn walked into the bathroom to brush her teeth. She would try to sleep, but she didn't know how successful she would be. Every time she turned around, she was finding more questions and not enough answers.

A rainstorm came in with a ferocious blast, lightning, thunder, and wind rattling the windows. Evelyn woke up suddenly, her heart pounding. It took a few seconds for her to realize it was just the storm that had awakened her. She tried to fall back to sleep, but her mind wouldn't let her rest.

Usually, she loved sleeping while it rained, but not tonight when her mind was full of secret passageways, ghost sightings, theft, and lies.

Evelyn tossed and turned through the night and, in the morning, she felt horrible. Her eyes were gravelly, her head hurt, and she was out of sorts. She knew she needed to apologize to Shelby, but she didn't know how her niece would respond. Would they get into another fight? Would Shelby ignore her?

She shared her feelings with James moments before he left for work, and he said, "It doesn't matter how Shelby responds. If you feel the Lord nudging you to apologize, you should."

Evelyn had to agree with him.

With that in mind, she knocked on Shelby's door after James left for work. "Good morning," she said. "Can I come in?"

There was no answer. Evelyn slowly turned the knob and entered Shelby's room, but she wasn't there, and all her clothes had been picked up. Had she gone downstairs to do her laundry?

For a long time, Evelyn stood and stared at the closed closet door. Was Shelby hiding something? What if it was the coin? All

Evelyn needed to do was open the doors and have a look. If she found the coin, her worries about it would be put to rest—though it would begin a series of unfortunate events in Shelby's life.

Taking a step into the room, Evelyn hesitated.

She couldn't invade Shelby's privacy—no matter how much she wanted to find the coin. Either she believed Shelby or she didn't. If she broke Shelby's trust and violated her privacy, their relationship was as good as over—what little was left.

Evelyn slowly backed out of Shelby's room and closed the door. She had no solid proof that Shelby was guilty, and she wouldn't search her things.

Instead, Evelyn went downstairs and found Shelby sitting at the kitchen counter, eating a bowl of cereal.

"Good morning," Evelyn said. "It's nice to see you up so early."

Shelby shrugged and took a bite of her cereal.

"Did you get some laundry started?"

"Yeah." Shelby spoke with her mouth full. "I like how your detergent smells."

Evelyn walked to the coffee maker, a smile lifting her lips at the rare compliment. She went about making her cup of coffee and then began cooking her morning bowl of oatmeal.

"I want to apologize for last night," Evelyn said as she set the water to boil on the stove. "I've asked you about the coin several times, and I shouldn't have brought it up again."

Shelby lifted a shoulder but didn't meet Evelyn's eyes. "Whatever."

Evelyn walked across the kitchen to stand in front of Shelby. "The last thing I want to do is hurt you."

"You didn't hurt me."

That was clearly what Shelby would like Evelyn to believe—what she probably wanted the whole world to believe. No doubt she wanted to be impervious to being hurt, by her mom, her dad, her boyfriend…her aunt.

"I made you upset," Evelyn said, "and, for that, I'm sorry."

Shelby finally looked up at Evelyn and studied her for a couple of seconds, her barriers coming down—if only momentarily. "Okay."

It didn't take long for the water to boil, so Evelyn poured in her oats, ready to change the subject. "What do you plan to do today?"

Another shrug.

Shelby finished her cereal and put her bowl in the sink before leaving the kitchen.

"Have a good day," Evelyn called out.

After eating her oatmeal, Evelyn left the house and walked to Mercy. The rain had stopped, but the sky was still dark and menacing. Evelyn could have asked Joy to give her a ride, but Joy usually went to work before Evelyn. If it was really bad later, James would come and pick her up.

But for now, the weather matched Evelyn's mood.

She entered the hospital at exactly seven o'clock and went right to the museum. Shirley and Joy were standing outside the door, chatting, when Evelyn approached.

"No Anne?" Evelyn asked.

"I have a feeling she stayed in bed." Shirley wore a pair of white scrubs with pink and purple flowers. Her ponytail band was white with a purple print that matched the work outfit perfectly. She held a steaming mug of coffee and yawned. "Mama scolded me this morning for coming in so late last night." Shirley took care of her mother,

Regina, who lived with her. Regina, who worked many years as a nurse at Mercy, was a favorite at the hospital. "I felt like I was back in high school getting caught coming in after curfew."

Joy smiled. "That's one good thing about living alone. No one to answer to."

Evelyn unlocked the museum door and flipped on the light switch.

Since the police had released the crime scene, the team of curators had been doing an amazing job pulling the exhibits together. Gone were the piles of boxes and totes, and in their place were top-notch displays.

"It's like a whole new room," Shirley said as she stopped to look at a display. From early stethoscopes to blood-letting kits, the items were under plexiglass covers and had the proper plaques nearby to describe what the visitors were looking at. "I'm excited to get in here when it's finished and really study everything."

"Right now," Evelyn said, "we have about an hour to scout around and see if we can find a passageway."

"Don't you think the construction workers would have found one, if there was one to find?" Joy asked.

"Not necessarily. There are parts of this room that were left untouched, especially over there." Evelyn pointed to one of the main structural walls, near the plastic area where Adam worked with the artifacts. The wall was made of the original dark red brick.

"Well," Shirley said, "let's start there."

"What are we looking for?" Joy asked as she followed Evelyn to the plastic walls.

"I don't know." Evelyn lifted her hands. "A trapdoor, a false front, anything, really. The passageway in the Vault was hidden under a heavy desk for decades. There's no telling where there might be more."

After the earlier secret passageway was found, Evelyn wondered how many other tunnels or rooms might be hiding in between the walls or under the floors of Mercy Hospital. Would they soon find another?

The women worked quietly as they pushed and prodded. Evelyn moved behind the plastic. They had put the workspace here, since it would require the least amount of remodeling in the whole museum.

Evelyn had to turn on her cell phone flashlight to see in this area. It was dark and claustrophobic, but she knew she could easily get out if she needed to. She pushed aside the plastic hanging from the ceiling as she pressed her hands along the wall. It was frustrating, not knowing what—if anything—she would find.

As she moved, she felt the wood floor beneath her feet hollow out. Her heels made a different sound as she stepped back and forth over the space. She paused and bent to knock on the wood. It sounded different in this area as opposed to a couple of feet away.

"Joy, Shirley," Evelyn called out to them. "I think I might have found something."

"Where are you?" Joy called.

"Over here, behind the plastic wall."

Her friends pushed aside the plastic and found Evelyn.

"Here," she said as she tapped the floor, pushing against the boards to see if she could find a loose one—and she did! The board popped out of place, revealing a latch.

Evelyn's eyes opened wide, and she looked up at Shirley and Joy.

"I think you just discovered how the thief got into the museum without being detected," Shirley said.

"Well done, Evelyn." Joy grinned.

Evelyn handed her phone to Shirley. "The next question is, who knows about this passageway? And why did they use it to take just the coin? They could have taken a lot more." She looked from the latch to her friends. "Should I open it?"

"Yes." Shirley's voice was filled with curiosity. "If you don't, I will."

"Okay." Evelyn pulled the latch. It was rusty and old, but it came loose, and she was able to lift the whole trapdoor. An iron ladder descended down to a room below. The floor was dirt, but the walls were made of the same red brick.

"It doesn't look like a big room," Shirley said, flashing the light down the opening. "Maybe seven feet high."

"Should we check it out?" Evelyn wasn't sure. "What if someone is in there?"

"If it's a passageway," Joy said, "and they heard us, whoever is down there is surely on their way out."

"Good point." Evelyn was anxious to find where this led—if anywhere. "Who wants to go with me?"

Shirley nodded, but Joy didn't look so sure. "How about I wait up here, in case someone comes in. We wouldn't want anyone locking us down there."

"Okay." Evelyn didn't wait another moment. She took her phone from Shirley and positioned herself on the ladder to begin her descent into the dark room. Shirley pulled out her phone and used the flashlight to help Evelyn navigate. Thankfully, Evelyn was wearing a pair of slacks and a loose blouse, which made it easier for her to move. But it was still eerie to enter an underground space she'd never been in before.

When she reached the floor, she flashed her light around to get her bearings.

The room was about ten feet square, with nothing but cobwebs and dust. If something had been in there before, it was long gone.

"Well?" Joy asked as Shirley started down the ladder.

"It's empty." Evelyn pointed the light in one corner. "But there is a tunnel."

When Shirley reached the room, she looked to Evelyn. "Should we explore?"

"Absolutely." Evelyn led the way to the tunnel. "We haven't come this far to turn back now."

"Be safe," Joy said. "We don't know how secure the tunnel is. What if it collapses?"

"It's made of brick." Evelyn reached up and touched the ceiling just a couple of inches above her head. "It looks pretty sound."

Her voice echoed in the dark chamber, coming back to her in a creepy cadence.

They moved through the tunnel, neither one saying a word. It was dank and musty, but Evelyn continued on.

"Wait," Shirley said. "What's that?"

Evelyn looked toward the floor where Shirley had pointed her light.

A flash of metal caught Evelyn's eye. She bent to look closer and discovered it was a necklace with a delicate silver chain and a pendent made up of three circles, two gold and one silver, all intertwining to make a sphere.

"This looks new," Shirley said as she picked it up. "The clasp is broken."

"It's not dusty or rusted," Evelyn agreed. "Whoever lost it was down here recently."

"Maybe it belongs to our thief." Shirley handed the necklace to Evelyn, and she put it into her pocket.

They continued to follow the tunnel.

Eventually, they came to a small wooden door. It was here, in the dirt, that Evelyn noticed the most footprints. There were a few different ones, all messed up together. "Do you think this leads outside?" she asked Shirley as she turned the knob on the door.

"Let's find out."

It took a lot of work, but Evelyn was able to pull the door open—and when she did, she frowned. "It's another tunnel."

"Maybe it connects with the one that goes into the Vault."

Evelyn bit her bottom lip. "I'm not sure if we should keep exploring. I'd like to get Seamus down here to take a look. I definitely think whoever took the coin used the tunnel—but whether it was Shelby, Dr. Langer, or the Queenie imposter, it's impossible to tell."

"At least we found the necklace. That might tell us something."

"Come on," Evelyn said. "Let's go tell Joy what we found. I need to talk to the custodial staff and see if anyone else in the hospital knows about this passage."

"What about the other branch of the tunnel?"

"We'll have to deal with that later. Right now, I need some answers."

The passageway was the first lead Evelyn had discovered since the coin incident began. Now she could prove that she and Shelby weren't the only people who could have been in the museum the night the coin was taken.

But it still didn't tell her who was responsible for its theft.

Chapter Twelve

EVELYN WAITED UNTIL AFTER EIGHT to let Adam and his team into the museum before she went to the basement to talk to Earl and Oscar. She didn't mention the secret passageway to Adam, not wanting to tip her hand, in case he knew about it and was somehow responsible for the coin's disappearance. At this point, anyone connected to the coin was still a suspect, and she didn't want everyone to know that she was aware of the passageway.

Evelyn would also need to talk to Seamus and tell him about this discovery so he and his team could take the proper security measures necessary to keep the building safe.

But, at this point, Evelyn had a feeling that the passageway would be useful in helping to apprehend the thieves, because she was pretty sure that more than one person was responsible for the theft. Seeing the two people last night and then all the footprints in the dirt floor near the door made it clear.

Stopping in at the records department, Evelyn told Stacia where she was going and promised that when she was done, she would devote the rest of the workday to her job. Stacia was doing great picking up the slack, but Evelyn didn't expect her to continue. She did ask Stacia to do a little more investigating into the person who had uploaded the two videos of Queenie Bennett. Maybe he had left a clue that might point to his identity.

It was a busy Wednesday at Mercy Hospital as Evelyn left the records department and made her way to one of the service doors near the security offices. The hospital hummed with the conversation and business of visitors, patients, and staff. Evelyn marveled that so much activity could be going on around her and no one knew that she had found a secret passageway and was trying to uncover a troubling mystery. With only ten days until the grand opening, she was running out of time. They needed to find the coin and get it back into its case, because the last thing she wanted when the governor of South Carolina came to visit was an unsolved investigation under way—with her being one of the main suspects.

Evelyn pushed open the door and took the steps down into the lowest level. It was loud here, since the laundry was also housed in the basement. Large dryers hummed, and steam hissed from boilers. Bypassing the laundry, Evelyn walked to the custodial office and opened the door.

Earl was sitting at his desk, on the phone, and Oscar was at his desk, working on his computer. They were alone in the room, and they both looked up at Evelyn when she entered.

With a quick wave of his hand and a bright smile, Earl acknowledged Evelyn and indicated that he needed a minute to finish his call.

Oscar, on the other hand, didn't even bother to nod a greeting or smile at her arrival. He simply looked back at his computer as if she hadn't arrived. His reputation in Mercy wasn't a great one. He was known as a quiet man who did his job well but who didn't like to be questioned or criticized. For the most part, people gave Oscar a wide berth.

Taking a seat across from Earl's desk, Evelyn tried not to pay attention to the call he was taking. It sounded like a sales call, since Earl was telling the person on the other end that he needed to purchase two hundred. Though, two hundred of what, Evelyn didn't know.

"You'll get that here within the week?" Earl asked. "Great. Thanks for returning my call. Goodbye." He hung up and gave Evelyn his full attention. "It's nice to see you back here so soon."

His bright smile, coupled with his white hair and beard, made Evelyn feel welcome and comfortable.

"What can I do for you today?" Earl asked.

"It's about the museum," Evelyn said, glancing quickly at Oscar to see how he reacted to her statement.

The man continued to stare at his computer, but Evelyn saw the faintest hint of tension around his mouth.

"We haven't started our nightly cleaning in there," Earl said. "We're waiting for the curators to finish their work, and then we'll come in for one deep clean the day before the grand opening." He pulled out his schedule and showed her where he had written a few notes. "After the museum is open to the public, we'll go in nightly and vacuum, remove garbage, wash down the plexiglass display cases, and dust when necessary."

"That sounds perfect," Evelyn said. "I appreciate your willingness to take on another space—but that's not why I've come."

"Oh?" Earl closed his schedule and steepled his hands on his desk. "Something else I can help with?"

"This information needs to stay between us, for now." She looked at Oscar again—and this time he met her gaze. "I just discovered a trapdoor in the museum and a secret passageway that connects to another tunnel."

Warren's bushy white eyebrows rose high on his head. "Seriously?"

"Yes. I think that the people responsible for the coin's disappearance used the passage to get in and out of the museum without being noticed."

"That's remarkable," Earl said. "We're aware of the other tunnel, the one that leads into the Vault. It's locked, and the entrance from outside is hidden behind a hedge."

"How do you know the thieves used the passageway?" Oscar asked, his full attention on Evelyn now. "That sounds like a big assumption."

"Last night I was reminded of the passageway we found under the Vault, so I went looking for one today in the museum. I found it in the corner, under a trapdoor. It's the only thing that makes sense. Someone got into the museum and left without being spotted by the video surveillance."

"Did you enter it?" Earl asked.

"I did. Shirley Bashore and I followed it until it came to a door, leading to another tunnel."

Earl's face betrayed his surprise and curiosity. "How many tunnels are down there?"

"I'm not sure. I came here first, to see if anyone knows about this other passageway."

"I was just aware of the one," Earl said. "I had no idea there were more."

"None of your custodial staff knows about it either?"

"If they do, no one's mentioned it to me." Earl turned and looked at Oscar. "Have you heard of this particular passageway before?"

"Can't say that I have." He frowned. "Where did you say you found the trapdoor?"

"In the corner, behind the plastic walls of Adam's workstation. There was a loose board, and when I pulled it up, I found a latch."

"Would you mind showing it to me?" Earl asked. "I'd be interested in getting a look."

"Sure. I'm going to call Seamus too," Evelyn said. "I'd like security to come and look at it."

"How about we meet there in thirty minutes or so?" Earl asked.

"That'll work," Evelyn agreed. "But could we please keep this between us? I don't want anyone else knowing about the passageway at this point. It could compromise the investigation."

"Of course," Earl said. "We won't say a word to anyone outside this room."

"Thank you." Evelyn stood to leave and caught a glimpse of Oscar out of the corner of her eye. He had grabbed his cell phone and was furiously typing.

He looked up at her, his fingers growing still over the keypad of his phone. For a couple of seconds, he just stared at her and then turned his back and kept typing.

Maybe it was time to figure out where Oscar Maverick was the night of the theft.

Thirty minutes later, Evelyn had Seamus and Rafe Jagger, another security officer who had been at Mercy for less than a year, in her wake as they approached the museum entrance. Adam looked up from his work on an exhibit, a question in his eyes.

"Something wrong?" he asked as he put down the screwdriver in his hand and stepped away from his work cart.

Evelyn glanced at Seamus, who had convinced her they would need to let Adam know about the secret passageway. Since he was working in such close proximity to the trapdoor and he was in charge of the team of curators, he had the right to know.

"Can we speak to you privately?" Evelyn asked, indicating that they go to the corner, near his workstation.

"Sure."

He followed her as she lifted one edge of the plastic and entered the dust-free space.

Seamus and Rafe were close behind. Earl and Oscar must have come in shortly after them, because they also joined Evelyn.

All five men looked to her as she addressed Adam. "Early this morning I discovered a secret passageway that leads from another tunnel to this room." She pointed at the spot in the corner where she had found the trapdoor. "It's under the boards there."

Adam's eyes bulged behind his glasses at the news. "Are you serious?"

Evelyn nodded.

"Wow." Adam shook his head. "How cool that there's been a hidden tunnel right here under our noses this whole time."

"I think we should figure out where the other branch of the tunnel goes," Evelyn said. "If someone's been using it, we need to be sure to barricade all possible entries and exits to keep the rest of our artifacts safe."

"I agree," Seamus said. "Can you show us the trapdoor?"

Evelyn led them back to the spot where she had discovered the passageway. She removed the board and opened the latch.

Seamus, Rafe, Earl, and Oscar all had industrial-sized flashlights, which they used as they began to climb down the ladder. Earl let Evelyn follow Seamus and Rafe. She felt much safer surrounded by all these people than when it was just her and Shirley entering the tunnels earlier.

When all six of them were in the small room at the foot of the ladder, Evelyn felt claustrophobic. It wasn't a big room—and it was much smaller filled with so many people.

Seamus pointed his flashlight toward the opening.

"This tunnel extends for about thirty feet until you reach the door connecting it to the other tunnel," Evelyn said.

"Let's take a look." Seamus led the way. "Watch your step."

"And your head," Rafe commented, since he was the tallest one of the group.

Evelyn was sandwiched between the security guards and the custodians. She and Adam were right in the middle.

She had told Seamus about the necklace she'd found earlier, but he suggested she keep that information to herself for now. She still wasn't sure if Adam or someone from maintenance had anything to do with the coin's disappearance, and she wasn't about to give away all the clues she'd gathered. Besides, it was clearly a woman's necklace. She suspected it belonged to the woman playing Queenie—but who was she? Could Earl, Adam, or Oscar be the man recording her? Evelyn hadn't been able to get a good look at his face, so it was possible.

Finally, they came to the door at the end of the tunnel. Seamus opened it and flashed his light one way and then the other. "I think this is the tunnel that leads to the Vault."

The others followed him through the door, which wasn't very big, and into the shaft.

"A false front," Rafe said as he looked at the back of the door, which was covered in brick and would have been almost impossible to spot if the door had been closed.

"No wonder we didn't know about it." Seamus pointed his flashlight to the right. "If we go this way we should be at the outside opening."

They all followed him. It didn't take long to come to the outlet, a door that was even smaller than the others, about two feet by two feet.

"This should open to the outside," Seamus said. "It's hidden behind a tall hedge."

"So whoever used it didn't just stumble on it," Evelyn said. "They had to have known it existed, and that there was another secret door leading from this tunnel to the museum."

"Exactly."

The room they were standing in felt damp and smelled musty. Evelyn might have been claustrophobic if her mind wasn't racing with possibilities. Had the Queenie imposter used this to get into the museum, to take the coin, and was she now cashing in on the publicity with the videos? Did she work at the hospital, perhaps? Did she know about the passageway? Or was she an employee at a museum who knew the history of the hospital and was aware of it that way?

"It looks like whoever used it resealed it," Rafe said. "But we'll have to look at getting this permanently closed off. We wouldn't want anyone else gaining access to the museum or the hospital this way."

"I agree." Evelyn nodded. "Apparently more people know about it than we realized."

"Thankfully, it doesn't appear to be a serious threat right now," Earl added.

"I definitely think this is how our suspect got into the museum unnoticed," Seamus said to Evelyn. "So it looks like you and your niece aren't necessarily the last people to have access to the museum the night the coin went missing."

Evelyn wanted to sigh in relief, but she knew that she still had a lot of unanswered questions. She had an idea how she might find some of the solutions, but she needed more help.

Chapter Thirteen

Evelyn shouldn't have taken a lunch break, with all the work she had facing her in the records department, but she needed an opportunity to talk with Joy, Anne, and Shirley after everything they had discovered that morning—and to discuss her idea. They had all agreed to meet for lunch in the hospital coffee shop earlier that day and she didn't want to back out on them.

The air was thick with the threat of rain as Evelyn entered the busy coffee shop. She was a little late because she'd waited for Stacia to return from her lunch break, but she knew exactly what she wanted to eat, so she didn't waste any time looking over the menu. After placing her order for a chicken salad sandwich and a cup of coffee, she carried her food into the dining area on a tray.

Joy and Shirley were already there, sitting across from each other by one of the large windows overlooking the Grove. The walls were decorated with coffee photography, including pictures of steaming cups of java, mounds of coffee beans, and groups of people sitting together and laughing over their drinks.

Shirley had a salad and glass of iced tea, while Joy was eating a wrap and potato chips. Rain began to fall outside, casting large droplets on the cement and tapping against the windowpanes. A couple of people who had opted to sit in the Grove ran into the coffee shop, laughing and shaking the rain off their clothes.

"Hi," Shirley said as Evelyn took a seat next to her.

Evelyn smiled at her in greeting. She didn't want to jump right into her idea, since Anne was not there yet. Instead, the women spent the first few minutes chatting about their families and about the odds and ends of their lives.

When Anne finally appeared with a salad, she slipped into the spot beside Joy, an apology on her lips. "I'm sorry I didn't come in earlier and help you look for the secret passageway. I was so exhausted this morning when my alarm clock went off, I knew I needed to get more sleep." Anne looked at Evelyn with hope in her face. "Did you have any success?"

"We did." Evelyn smiled. "And don't worry about not joining us, Anne. I completely understand."

"Oh, good." She rearranged herself in the seat, her eyes filled with curiosity. "Tell me what you found."

"There is a trapdoor in the museum," Evelyn said quietly, not wanting anyone else to hear. "With a tunnel that leads to the tunnel that goes to the Vault." She looked at Joy and Shirley. "I have a feeling that whoever took the coin used the passageway—and my gut is telling me it's probably the Queenie imposter. What if she's an employee here at the hospital who knows about the tunnel?"

"I suppose that's a possibility," Shirley agreed.

"I didn't see another video uploaded today from Queenie or her videographer," Evelyn continued, "which means that we interrupted their plans last night. They'll probably be out again tonight, trying to get another recording. I'm thinking we need to do another stakeout."

The three of them stared at Evelyn for a moment, but it was Shirley who said, "Are you serious?"

"Very." Evelyn not only wanted the coin back because it was irreplaceable, but because it impacted her job, her family, and her friends. "I need to know who the Queenie imposter is. If she's an employee here, then it would be easy to link her to the tunnel and the theft."

"Maybe you should ask Seamus to do the stakeout with us," Shirley suggested.

"Us?" Evelyn's excitement grew. "Are you in?"

She shrugged and chuckled. "What's another night without sleep? I am kind of curious to see how it all plays out. Maybe Seamus wouldn't mind joining us. After all, if we are able to confront this imposter, wouldn't it be nice to have a security guard there?"

"I'll see what he has to say," Evelyn said. "He might think we're more trouble than we're worth."

Shirley laughed, her brown eyes filling with merriment. "He wouldn't be the first person to accuse me of that."

Evelyn was about to take a bite of her sandwich but remembered the other piece of information she wanted to talk to her friends about. "I had Stacia try to discover who uploaded the videos of Queenie, but she hasn't had any luck. Both are under different accounts, and neither one has the name of the person listed."

"And you didn't get a good look at them last night?" Anne asked.

"It was too dark." Evelyn sighed. "Our only hope is catching them in the act."

Anne reached out and patted Evelyn's arm. "Hopefully that's exactly what you'll do."

When the four of them had finished lunch and gone their separate ways, Evelyn stopped in at the security office to see if Seamus was there. Thankfully, he was sitting at his desk.

"More paperwork?" Evelyn asked with a smile when he saw her enter.

"I guess it's the trouble I get for being the department head—but then, you're familiar with that, I suppose."

"Too familiar." Evelyn couldn't help but add, "We have such great staff members working with us, though. I don't know what I would do without my team."

"Same here." Seamus put aside his paperwork and gave Evelyn his full attention. "What can I do for you?"

"I have an idea and I need to run it by you."

"Shoot."

"I'm having a hard time finding information on the two people making Queenie videos. Right now, they're our best suspects. I was thinking the only way we might be able to find out who they are and question them is if we do another stakeout tonight."

Seamus seemed to be thinking about the idea and then slowly started to nod. "Might not be a bad idea. I don't know how many guards I have at my disposal, though. I'd have to call in some extra help."

"Shirley Bashore and I would gladly volunteer. She was with me last night and this morning and is happy to do what she can."

Seamus studied Evelyn for a few moments, as if weighing the risk in having her and Shirley there. "Are you sure you're up to it?"

"Absolutely. I have the most to lose or gain in this situation, and I'm willing to do whatever it takes."

Finally, Seamus agreed. "Okay. I'll see who I can pull together. You said they showed up after midnight last night?"

"About twelve thirty."

"Then it doesn't pay to get here too early. Let's meet in my office at eleven. Does that work?"

"Sure."

"I'll make a plan and let you know what I decide when everyone arrives."

"Perfect. Thanks for your help." Evelyn left the security office and headed back to Records. Her lips felt dry, so she patted her pocket to see where she had put her lip balm and felt the necklace there.

In all the excitement of the day, she'd completely forgotten about the little clue they had found in the tunnel. It was too late to call her friends back together to show the necklace to them, and she didn't think it mattered all that much, since they were about to apprehend the suspects that evening.

She'd hold on to it and return it to its owner when they had her in custody.

The thought put a smile on Evelyn's face.

Moonlight shimmered across the harbor, glistening on the waves as they rolled toward the seawall not too far from Mercy Hospital. Evelyn and Shirley had been stationed around the corner from the angel statue, close to where the couple had outrun them the night before, while Seamus, Rafe, and another guard were positioned at various points around the Grove. If the couple returned to the angel statue to continue recording, they would be surrounded and would have nowhere to run.

It was cool, with a northeasterly breeze coming off the Atlantic. Evelyn wore a cardigan, and she pulled it closer to herself. The night was quiet, with only the sound of the waves to break up the silence. Shirley kept her thoughts to herself as she sat on one of the canvas folding chairs they had brought.

Evelyn glanced at her phone and saw that it was half-past midnight. Nothing but the ocean had stirred for the hour and a half they had been at their post.

Boredom wrapped around Evelyn. Her hair kept blowing in her face, and she constantly had to slip it back behind her ears. But it was the fatigue that bothered her the most. With less than five hours of sleep the night before, she was exhausted. A short nap at home after supper helped, but it almost made her feel more tired.

Worse, Shelby hadn't taken her clothes out of the washing machine, so Evelyn had to do it for her before she could get a load of laundry done. Her lack of sleep and worry over the coin had started to get the best of her, and she lost her temper with her niece. Shelby went to her room and refused to come out for supper. When Evelyn left the house, she didn't even say goodbye to Shelby, knowing they both needed their space.

Now, as she sat near the harbor with nothing to do but think, Evelyn cringed to remember how she had reacted to Shelby. The last thing her niece needed was another impatient, selfish adult to yell at her. Though it was hard, she needed to be as calm and forbearing as possible. Shelby needed someone she could trust to draw her out and listen. The weekend would soon be upon them, and Evelyn hoped to use it as a time to do something special with Shelby—even if she had to drag her out of the house. She would focus all of her attention on her niece—and if the coin thieves were captured tonight, they'd have a lot to celebrate.

"What time is it?" Shirley asked Evelyn quietly as she yawned. "It has to be at least one."

"Twelve thirty-five," Evelyn whispered.

Shirley groaned and burrowed deeper into the blanket she had around her shoulders. "I'm afraid we might not see them again. We probably scared them off last night."

"I don't know." Evelyn needed to believe they were about to capture the couple responsible for the theft. "The lure of more money for their YouTube videos is probably worth the risk."

"I hope you're right."

A soft sound met Evelyn's ears. It was like the whisper of slippers against fabric. As it grew louder, Evelyn realized it was the sound of crinoline—and it was coming from a young woman in a billowing gown, walking toward the statue.

Evelyn reached out and grasped Shirley's arm.

It was dark, but the moon was bright, and Evelyn's eyes had already adjusted. She was able to recognize a man as he came up behind the woman—and, if she wasn't mistaken, it was the same guy from last night.

Her heart beat hard as she saw Rafe take a step away from his hiding spot. Seamus and the other guard followed, and Evelyn and Shirley joined them.

"Hold it right there," Rafe said. "You're surrounded, so it doesn't pay to run."

"Whoa," the guy said as he put up his hands.

"We didn't do anything wrong," the woman said.

For a second, Evelyn just stared—but then her eyes opened wide and her mouth fell. "Shelby?"

Chapter Fourteen

SHELBY SHIFTED HER GAZE TO Evelyn, her eyes growing twice their size. "Aunt Evelyn?"

It was Shelby, in a wig. Evelyn couldn't believe what she was seeing.

"It *was* you," Evelyn said, taking a step toward her niece. "This whole time, it was you. How could you lie to me?"

"I didn't lie." Shelby swallowed and took a step back, clearly upset that she had been caught.

"Do you know this woman?" Seamus asked.

Evelyn nodded. "She's my niece."

"And him?" Seamus asked, pointing at the guy with Shelby.

Evelyn looked closer. His sharp nose, small mustache, and dark hair were all-too familiar. "You must be Rodney."

No one said a word, and then finally, Shelby said, "Rodney, this is my aunt, the one I'm staying with."

"Hey," Rodney said.

Evelyn's chest constricted with anger and pain as she shook her head. "I can't believe you'd do this to me, Shelby."

"Do what?" Shelby asked. "I didn't do anything to you."

"How could you have taken the coin? And, worse, lied to me about it."

"For the last time," Shelby said between gritted teeth, "I did not. Take. The. Coin."

"Then what is all this?" Evelyn asked, not trying to disguise her frustration or disappointment. "Do you think I was born yesterday? You knew about the secret passageway, and you used it to take the coin. Now you're trying to make a buck with these ridiculous videos."

Shelby's nostrils flared. "I didn't take that stupid coin, and I have no idea what passageway you're talking about."

"How can I believe you after you've lied to me this whole time?" Evelyn had been such a fool, hoping Shelby was innocent all week.

"You're going to have to, because I have no idea where that coin is. Rodney and I are just having fun. We haven't hurt anything."

"You're trespassing on hospital property," Rafe said.

"Says who?" Rodney asked. "I thought all this space was open to the public. It's a hospital, isn't it?"

"We have visiting hours," Seamus said, taking a step closer to Rodney. "And they're over."

Evelyn felt sick and embarrassed. She'd been so convinced of Shelby's innocence that she had put her career and reputation on the line for her.

"How many times have you snuck out of the house?" Evelyn asked Shelby.

Shelby cast her gaze to the sidewalk and shrugged, her voice small. "Every night."

Evelyn just shook her head, irritated at herself for assuming the best.

Seamus stood with his feet planted and his arms crossed. She felt his gaze on her, but she couldn't meet his eyes.

"This is Rodney Fletcher," Evelyn said to Seamus. "He's been getting my niece into trouble for quite a while now."

Rodney shook his head and lifted his hands. "We made a couple of videos. Big deal. Where's the crime in that?"

"Did you take the coin?" Seamus asked.

"No." Rodney met his direct gaze.

"Is that true?" Seamus asked Shelby.

"Yes."

Seamus took a few breaths before he turned to Evelyn. "All they're guilty of is impersonating a ghost. There's not a lot I can do about it."

Evelyn still had the necklace in her pocket. She pulled it out now and showed it to Shelby but didn't say anything.

Shelby looked at the necklace and then at Evelyn, zero recognition in her face.

"Is this yours?" Evelyn asked her.

"No."

"Are you sure?"

"Have you ever seen me wear an old lady's necklace—or any jewelry?"

Evelyn couldn't recall seeing a single piece of jewelry on her niece. If she had worn the necklace into the passageway, wouldn't Evelyn have seen it on her at some point before that?

"What do you want to do?" Seamus asked Evelyn.

With a sigh, Evelyn said, "I'll take Shelby home. We have a lot to talk about."

"And what about this guy?" he asked, pointing at Rodney.

Evelyn shrugged. She preferred not to see Rodney again.

"I want your contact information," Seamus said to him. "And then I want you to go back to wherever you came from. Got it?"

Rodney pressed his lips together and shrugged. "Whatever, man."

Evelyn didn't wait for Shelby to say goodbye to her boyfriend. She took her by the arm and started to walk toward her waiting car, telling Shirley goodbye as she went.

Shirley gave her a weak smile.

There were a lot of questions Evelyn had for her niece, and she wasn't letting her go to bed before they had a long talk.

Neither Evelyn nor Shelby said a word as they drove home. Evelyn was afraid that if she said something without giving herself time to bring her thoughts and emotions under control, she would regret it.

And she wanted James by her side as she addressed the issues they needed to face. Shelby had pushed Evelyn to her limits of patience and goodwill, and things needed to change drastically. James would add his wisdom and common sense to the conversation.

Shelby turned to look at Evelyn. "Aunt Ev—"

"Don't." Evelyn took a right. "I'm not ready."

With a groan of frustration, Shelby crossed her arms and looked back out the window.

Evelyn pulled into the drive and turned off the engine. Shelby climbed from the car and started toward the house.

"Don't go to your room," Evelyn called out to her. "We're going to have a nice long chat."

"Whatever. You're going to believe what you want to believe, so why even bother? Just tell me what you think you need to say, and I'll go pack my bags."

It was dark and late. The last thing Evelyn wanted was to disturb their neighbors. She walked around Shelby and found her house key. "You don't need to pack your bags," she said quietly. "I have several questions I want you to answer with complete honesty. I intend to listen very carefully."

She unlocked the door and flipped on the living room light. The ornate fireplace and white furniture usually made Evelyn feel a sense of calm and comfort but not tonight.

"Have a seat," she said to Shelby. "I'm going to wake James."

Shelby shook her head and rolled her eyes. "So you can tell him what a horrible person I am? And how I did such terrible things with Rodney—things you've assumed?"

"I want James here so he and I can both hear what you have to say."

With a sigh, Shelby threw herself onto the sofa.

Evelyn walked down the hallway to the stairs. Her emotions were still a jumbled mess of disappointment, frustration, anger, and fear. By the time she arrived at their bedroom, tears had even sprung to her eyes, despite her best effort to keep them at bay.

"Evie?" James asked as he reached over and flipped on his bedside lamp. He took one look at her and sat up in bed. "What's wrong? What happened?"

"It's Shelby." Evelyn swallowed the emotions and impatiently wiped the tear that had escaped her eye. "We caught her tonight with her boyfriend. She's been sneaking out with him every night and impersonating Queenie Bennett."

James got out of bed. "Where is she now?"

"In the living room, waiting to talk to us."

"And where is her boyfriend?"

"I don't know—but I hope he's on his way back to Jacksonville. I know he's the reason she's been getting into all this trouble."

"Now, don't give her such an easy out. She's been making her own decisions all along, and she needs to take responsibility for her actions." He took Evelyn's hand and stepped into his slippers. "Let's go talk to her and see what we can figure out. Nothing's broken that can't be fixed."

"Are you sure? What if she sold the coin already—or lost it? How in the world will I ever make that right?"

"None of this is your fault, Evelyn. If she took the coin, she will have to deal with the consequences. Try to relax and focus on this moment. We'll deal with the rest when the time comes—if it comes. We need to give her the benefit of the doubt."

"I have been," Evelyn said. "And look where that's gotten us. She said she's snuck out of the house every night since she arrived. Every night, James, even when she gave her word she wouldn't. Who knows what other trouble she's been in? And how am I going to trust her after this? I know she's hurting, but how can I help someone I don't trust or believe?"

"If she's contrite—if she asks for your forgiveness—then there's hope. We can move beyond this and still help her. Sometimes we have to hit rock bottom before we can start to climb back up."

Evelyn tried to accept the things he was saying, knowing he was right. James was always able to be a voice of reason when Evelyn struggled with her emotions. She would choose to believe him—and choose to hope that not all was lost for Shelby.

"Are you ready to talk to her?" James asked, opening the bedroom door.

Evelyn nodded and followed him back downstairs and into the living room. She half expected to find Shelby gone, but she was still sitting on the sofa, wearing the long gown. She had taken off the wig, and her blond hair was matted against her head. The wig was in a mess at her side, looking more like a large rat than a head of hair.

Shelby didn't look up when they came into the room. James and Evelyn took seats across from her.

Evelyn looked to James, hoping he'd take the lead. She was still a little too upset to trust herself to speak.

"I heard what happened this evening," James said to Shelby. "Care to explain it in your own words?"

Shelby shrugged. "You'll believe what you want to believe, so what's the point?"

"We want to hear what happened, from your point of view." His voice was so sincere, and so serious, Shelby finally looked up at him. "But we need the absolute truth from you, Shelby. No matter what. Do you understand?"

She studied him for a moment and then nodded. She wasn't wearing any makeup, so her clear blue eyes looked wide and vulnerable.

Evelyn waited as Shelby swallowed and then said, "Rodney followed me from Jacksonville. He got here the day after me, so the first time I snuck out"—she looked at Evelyn with hurt in her gaze—"I didn't sneak into the hospital museum. I went to meet Rodney at an all-night diner. I was honest when I said I wasn't anywhere near the hospital. And I didn't take the coin."

Neither Evelyn nor James said anything for a moment. If what Shelby said was true, then there might be someone on staff at the diner who could corroborate her story and give her an alibi.

"So, now do you believe me when I say I didn't take the coin?" Shelby asked Evelyn.

"I do." Evelyn wasn't sure if she was relieved or not. "But I have other questions. Why did you decide to impersonate Queenie's ghost?"

Shelby looked down at her fingernails, which were short and painted blue. "Rodney told me to be on the lookout for a way to make some money. When I heard the story about Queenie Bennett, I thought it would be fun to pretend to be her." She picked at her nails. "When I mentioned it to Rodney, he found the dress and the wig at a secondhand store and came up with the idea to record it and upload it online. He said we should give it a try and see if we made any money."

"I thought you told me you wanted a break from Rodney," Evelyn said.

"I didn't know he was going to follow me to Charleston." Shelby bit her bottom lip as she seemed to work out some thoughts. "When I told you that, I was being honest. I wanted him to leave, but I didn't know how to ask him. I kind of wanted to get caught so he would be forced to leave."

"Do you think he's gone now?" James asked.

"Yeah. He usually runs the second it looks like trouble."

Evelyn studied Shelby for a moment. "There are a lot of reasons why you should stop seeing him, but I think the most important right now is that you seem to make really poor choices when you're with him."

"Yeah. I know."

"We truly want what's best for you, and once we clear your name with the testimony of a witness who saw you at the diner on the night the coin was taken, I don't think you'll need to worry about any other charges." Evelyn paused. "Unless you've done something else we're not aware of."

"No. Just snuck out and pretended to be Queenie. That was why I didn't want you looking in my closet the other night. I hid the dress and wig in there and knew you'd figure out what I was doing."

Evelyn breathed a sigh of relief. "I believe you."

"I haven't been honest with you." Shelby looked from Evelyn to James. "And I broke my word about not leaving the house at night. I'm sorry."

Tears sprang to Evelyn's eyes again. "I forgive you."

"So do I." James leaned forward and put his hand on Shelby's knee. "We love you and are here for you, no matter what has happened in the past."

Evelyn stood and went to sit beside her niece. "I know things can't be the same as they were when you were a child, but I would really like to recapture some of the things we enjoyed together. Would you be willing to give it a try?"

The first hint of a smile lifted Shelby's lips. "I would."

"And we're going to make sure Rodney doesn't come back," James said. "Tomorrow, I'm going to call your dad and tell him what happened. We'll make sure Rodney stays as far away from you as possible. Okay?"

"Okay." Shelby's half smile turned to a full smile. "Thanks."

It wasn't a great way to start over, but Evelyn was willing to accept it, if it worked. She was relieved that Shelby was truly innocent of taking the coin, but it begged the question: Who *had* taken it? She had a feeling that if she could find the owner of the necklace, she would know who took the coin.

Though it wasn't much, it was still a clue. Tomorrow she would start looking for the owner in earnest.

Chapter Fifteen

The next morning, Evelyn walked down the stairs and found Shelby standing near the kitchen counter, folding a basket of laundry. She wore a pair of jean shorts and a T-shirt, with tennis shoes on her feet. Her hair looked freshly washed, and she had a little mascara on but no other makeup.

"Good morning," Evelyn said as she entered the kitchen for her daily coffee and oatmeal. "Thanks for getting the load out of the dryer."

Shelby didn't answer, but she gave Evelyn a half smile in response.

"Are you hungry?" Evelyn asked. "Would you like me to make you something?"

"I wouldn't mind some oatmeal, if you want to make enough for both of us."

"I'd be happy to make a double batch." Evelyn began the prep, hoping and praying that there had truly been a change in Shelby.

They both worked quietly for a couple of minutes while Evelyn set the water to boil and then filled a mug with coffee. When she was done, she joined Shelby at the counter to help her fold.

"I thought of something last night after you went to bed," Shelby said to Evelyn. "Something that might help you find out who took the coin."

Evelyn paused. "What?"

"Rodney and I weren't the only two people sneaking around the hospital at night this last week."

"You saw someone else?" Evelyn's pulse picked up speed. "Who?"

"I don't know who he was. It was the night we made our first video. We were looking at what we had filmed, near the hospital, when we heard someone coming. We were next to this tall hedge, close to the wall and it was really late, so it surprised us. The guy didn't see us, but he went behind the hedge and we got out of there."

"You're certain it was a man?"

"Yes."

"But you don't know which man?"

"He had a flashlight, pointed down, so I could see that he was wearing a uniform, but I didn't get a look at his face."

"What kind of uniform?" Evelyn tried to keep her voice calm and neutral, but this was the first real lead—beside the necklace—that she had. Shelby must be referring to the hedge that hid the tunnel opening.

"He was wearing a pair of jeans and a blue button-down shirt, tucked in at the waist. It was short-sleeved, and it had a patch with a name on the right side of his chest."

"Like a janitor's uniform?" Evelyn asked.

"Maybe."

Had one of the custodians been messing around with the tunnel? Which one? And why? If the man Shelby saw the day after the coin was taken was a custodian, then by the time Evelyn went to Earl and asked him about the tunnel, at least one of the men in his department knew about it. Did it pay to ask him again? Would he know the answer—or be willing to give it to her?

"Did you see anyone else?" Evelyn asked.

"No."

"Thanks for letting me know."

"Sure." Shelby continued to fold the laundry. For the first time since she'd arrived, there was something lighthearted about her. Maybe knowing that Rodney was gone and out of the picture, or that all her secrets were in the open, gave her a sense of freedom.

They ate their oatmeal together, discussing some of the places they might visit the coming weekend. It was Evelyn and James's wedding anniversary on Monday, and Evelyn mentioned that they were going to go out for supper with a few friends on Sunday night. When she asked Shelby if she'd care to join a handful of adults, she was surprised when Shelby said she would.

It was with a lighter step that Evelyn walked to work that morning. A quick call to the diner Shelby told them about confirmed that the waitress had seen Shelby and Rodney the night the coin was taken. Even though she still didn't know who took the coin, at least she knew for certain it wasn't Shelby.

When Evelyn opened the museum for Adam, he had a lot of questions about the passageway and what they had discovered. Since she still wasn't certain that he was innocent, she didn't give him too many details.

After opening the records department and getting a few things in order for the staff members to start their day, Evelyn finally had a chance to text Shirley, Anne, and Joy, asking them to meet her for lunch again. Since it was nice outside, she suggested they gather in the Grove, because she had something to show them.

The morning went quickly and soon it was twelve thirty. Evelyn left Records and went to the coffee shop. She ordered a cup of chicken noodle soup with ginger, which was purported to help fight the common cold, and met her friends in the Grove. They were sitting at their usual table, laughing and chatting when Evelyn joined them.

"Shirley already filled us in on what happened last night," Anne said as she put her hand on Evelyn's forearm. "I'm sorry to hear about Shelby."

"I hope you don't mind that I shared it," Shirley said.

"It's okay." Evelyn felt surprisingly relieved about the whole situation. "I was able to finally have an open conversation with her afterward. She gave me her alibi for the night the coin was taken, and it checked out."

"A tough situation," Anne said. "But I'm happy you now know for sure."

"Me too." Evelyn took the lid off her soup to let it cool. "But I called you all together to show you something Shirley and I found in the passageway yesterday. In all the commotion, I forgot about it."

"Oh," Shirley said. "I forgot too."

Evelyn pulled the silver and gold necklace from her pocket.

"A necklace?" Joy leaned forward. "It's pretty."

"It looks like it wasn't in the passageway for long," Evelyn said. "It's not rusted or tarnished."

"From what we can tell," Shirley volunteered, "the clasp is broken."

Anne also looked closely at the jewelry.

"Do any of you recognize it?" Evelyn asked.

Joy and Anne both shook their heads. Disappointment filled Evelyn's chest, but she refused to give up.

"Here comes Jerica," Shirley said.

Evelyn had almost forgotten about Jerica in all the fuss yesterday. "I was wondering when we might see her next."

"Evelyn!" Jerica stopped at their table. "I just heard they found the person pretending to be Queenie Bennett, but because she's a minor, they're not sharing her name. The man who helped her was caught, though, and they said his name was Rodney Fletcher. It didn't take me long on social media to figure out that he's your niece's boyfriend."

It didn't pay to respond, so Evelyn met Jerica's curious gaze with a slight smile.

"Is it true?" she asked.

"It's true that the man's name is Rodney." Evelyn shrugged. "I'm not at liberty to share any other information. There was no crime committed."

"Or was there?" Jerica took a seat next to Evelyn. "Did they get into the museum and steal the coin?"

"No." Evelyn felt crowded, but she moved over for Jerica to sit comfortably.

Jerica's gaze landed on the necklace, and she frowned. "What are you doing with Dr. Langer's jewelry?"

All four Mercy women stared at Jerica.

"You recognize this?" Evelyn asked.

"Yeah. It was the same one Dr. Langer was wearing the day she brought Blackbeard's medicine chest to the museum."

"How do you remember that?" Evelyn asked.

"Because I thought it was pretty."

Evelyn had been so concerned with the artifact, and then Shelby handling the coin, she hadn't been paying attention to what Dr. Langer was wearing.

"I wonder if there's a way we can prove it belongs to her before we confront her," Shirley said.

"You can see if she's wearing it in any of her pictures on social media," Jerica suggested.

"A great idea." Evelyn pulled out her cell phone and touched her Facebook icon. She didn't use social media often, but sometimes it came in handy.

"Hopefully she has a Facebook page," Joy said. "Not everyone likes social media."

"I love it." Jerica pulled out her phone. "I use it all the time." She tapped her screen a couple of times and then showed her pictures to them. "See, here I was on the night the coin was taken. My friends took me to Sullivan's Island Lighthouse. It was pretty cool. We stayed in this bed-and-breakfast." She showed them all the pictures, and it was the confirmation Evelyn needed to know that Jerica wasn't guilty of taking the coin.

Evelyn typed Sarah Langer's name into the search bar on Facebook, and her page immediately came up. "I found her."

"Do you see the necklace?" Joy asked.

Evelyn went to Dr. Langer's picture gallery and scrolled through all her photos. She didn't have many, and Evelyn found exactly what she was looking for.

“There!” She tapped the picture and enlarged the image with her fingers. “There it is.”

Sarah Langer was wearing the necklace in a picture she uploaded the day before the coin disappeared.

“I knew it,” Jerica said. “I bet she’s the one who stole the coin. Obviously she was in the tunnel.”

“Why would she do something like that?” Anne asked. “Isn’t she a historian?”

“Who knows why people do the things they do,” Evelyn said. “But now I know what I need to do.”

“What?” Jerica asked, her eyes gleaming with curiosity.

Maybe Evelyn wouldn’t share her plans openly—at least, not yet. Some things were better kept to herself.

Chapter Sixteen

Evelyn had to wait until the next day to execute her plan. It was nothing spectacular or clever, but she hoped it would help her find out if the necklace did, in fact, belong to Dr. Langer. And maybe, if all went well, she'd get Dr. Langer to admit that she'd been in the secret passageway and had taken the coin.

"Thank you for coming with me," Evelyn said to Joy, who had volunteered to accompany her to the Charleston Museum to confront the director.

"I'm happy to be here. I just wish I could have joined you and Shirley on the stakeout the other night."

Evelyn smiled at Joy as they walked to the museum on their lunch break. "I'm glad you're here now."

The massive brick building loomed ahead of them, shadows from the clouds passing over the facade in a strange sort of dance. Visitors were coming and going from the museum, and some were sitting on benches and tables in the courtyard eating their bag lunches. Birds hopped on the cement, picking at the crumbs, while a group of children in matching blue polo shirts ran and played in the yard.

"So," Joy said as they walked up the steps and entered the cool building, "what's the plan?"

Evelyn patted the necklace in her pocket. "I think a surprise visit is the best method to get her to tell the truth." She didn't bother to stop at the information desk this time but walked toward the back corner of the building where Dr. Langer's office was located. "But be prepared. Dr. Langer does not like me. Last time Shirley and I were here, she was pretty rude and dismissive. Now that I have the necklace and some proof that she was in the passageway, she's going to be even more belligerent."

"Will you tell her where you found it?"

"No. I want her to give us as much information as possible, so I won't feed any to her." Evelyn opened the door that led to the administrative department. The central part of the room was filled with cubicles, while a few offices lined one side. Dr. Langer's office was closest to the door.

"May I help you?" a woman asked as she stood up from her desk within a cubicle.

"We're here to see Dr. Langer," Evelyn said.

The woman smiled. "Dr. Langer isn't in her office right now. She's conducting a tour of the museum with a team of new hires."

"Oh." Evelyn hadn't anticipated this.

"Do you know when she'll be done?" Joy asked.

The woman looked at her wristwatch. "I'd say they're breaking for lunch right now, if this is a matter that can't wait."

"It's important we see her as soon as possible," Evelyn assured her. "Where might we find her?"

"They're probably in the staff lounge. It's across the museum on the other side of the lobby. I can take you there myself."

"We wouldn't want to put you out," Evelyn said.

"I was just heading there to eat my own lunch." The woman grabbed a thermal cooler from under her desk. "It's right this way."

Evelyn wasn't sure how upset Dr. Langer would be when they walked in on her eating lunch, but perhaps it could work to their benefit. The woman would be even more out of her element, especially with people around her. She might not be as confrontational as she had been in her office.

The lounge wasn't very large. Dr. Langer sat at a table with three individuals wearing forest-green polo shirts with the Charleston Museum logo on the left side. She had a can of Diet Coke in front of her, but she wasn't eating. Instead, she was visiting with the man on her left, who was eating a sandwich.

"There she is," the woman said as the three of them came to a stop in the lounge.

"Thank you for your help," Evelyn said. "Enjoy your lunch."

Dr. Langer looked up, and the expression on her face immediately changed. Her relaxed attitude shifted to suspicion and irritation. She rose from the table, excusing herself from the man she'd been speaking to, and approached them.

Evelyn braced herself, preparing for the attack. The woman was a force to be reckoned with.

"What are you doing here?" She looked at Joy. "And who is this?"

"This is my friend and coworker, Joy Atkins," Evelyn said. "Joy, this is Dr. Sarah Langer."

"It's nice to meet you," Joy said with a smile. She reached out her hand to shake Dr. Langer's, but the woman crossed her arms instead.

"You're not allowed in here," she said. "This room is for employees only."

"Is there somewhere we can talk?" Evelyn asked.

"Talk?" Dr. Langer scoffed. "I don't have anything to say to you. I thought I made that clear last time."

"I have something you might be interested in seeing," Evelyn said. "I can either show it to you in here or somewhere a little more private. It's up to you."

A few of the staff members had taken notice of the exchange, their curious glances cast toward them.

The woman looked over her shoulder and then lifted her chin. "Let's step out into the lobby."

Evelyn and Joy followed her through the door and into the vast lobby of the museum. It wasn't private, but it was empty except for the three of them.

"What's this about?" she asked, narrowing her eyes.

Evelyn pulled the necklace from her pocket. "I found this and was told that it belongs to you. It looks like real gold and silver, and I wanted to personally return it to you."

Dr. Langer looked at the necklace and immediately reached for it, her eyebrows tilting down into a frown. "Where did you find it?"

"At Mercy Hospital. It's yours, isn't it?"

As she held the necklace, her face softened, just a bit. "It is mine. My grandmother gave it to me before she passed away. I had no idea where I lost it. You found it in the museum?"

The passageway wasn't necessarily the same, but it was an extension of the museum. Evelyn didn't want to lie, but she didn't want to give away too much either. "When did you lose it?"

Dr. Langer's chin came up again, and her face hardened. "It's been gone for a month, at least. The clasp tends to break easily, so this isn't the first time I've lost it."

"That's strange," Evelyn said with a frown. "Jerica Dixon was the person who identified the necklace as yours, and she said she saw you wearing it the day you brought Blackbeard's medicine chest into the museum, less than two weeks ago. It's the only time she's seen you, so the necklace couldn't have been missing for a month."

"Oh," Dr. Langer said. "The days and weeks run together. Perhaps it hasn't been a month."

"Do you remember the last time you had it?" Evelyn asked.

She tucked the necklace into her pocket. "What business is it of yours?"

A group of visitors walked by, and the three of them remained silent for a moment. When they were gone, Evelyn said, "I found this necklace in a very strange place. It would help me if I knew when you might have lost it."

For a long time, Dr. Langer just stared at Evelyn, as if trying to ascertain what she might be suggesting.

When she finally spoke, she didn't appear to be so aloof or confident. Instead, she leaned in to speak quietly. "I was afraid it was stolen. It disappeared the very day I came to Mercy Hospital."

Evelyn glanced at Joy. Hadn't she just said she lost it? Now she was suggesting that it was stolen?

"Who do you think stole the necklace?" Joy asked.

"I couldn't say for sure. But I was afraid that whoever took it might use it to get me into trouble. That's what's happened, isn't it?

It was planted somewhere in Mercy Hospital to make me look guilty of a crime?"

Evelyn frowned, not believing her. "Who would want to get you into trouble?"

Dr. Langer swallowed and looked over her shoulder for a moment before saying, "Oscar Maverick."

"How do you know Oscar?" Evelyn was growing more confused by the moment.

"He's an old acquaintance of mine. A neighbor from my childhood. Believe me when I say that he has reason to hate me." She straightened her shoulders. "I turned down his advances several times, and this last time, he threatened me. He said he would make me suffer for refusing him." Her eyes were filled with apprehension. "That's what's happened, isn't it?" she asked again.

"I'm not sure." Evelyn was trying to wrap her mind around all this.

"I'm just thankful to have the necklace back," Dr. Langer said. "Thank you. I hope Oscar isn't in too much trouble."

Evelyn wasn't prepared to offer too much information, nor was she in a position to believe what she said.

"We're happy to help you with the necklace," she said.

Dr. Langer's face softened into the first smile Evelyn had received from her. It was a little unnerving. "If you need any more information about Oscar, please don't hesitate to come back."

"I don't know if that will be necessary." Evelyn smiled, though her lips were stiff and the gesture felt a little unnatural.

"Have a good day." She waved as Evelyn and Joy walked away.

"What do you make of that?" Joy asked Evelyn as they stepped out of the museum. "Something doesn't add up. I'm not sure I believe her."

"Same here." Evelyn led the way to Mercy Hospital. "But I know who we could talk to and find out if any of that is true."

"Oscar?"

"Exactly. Shelby told me she saw a man by the tunnel entrance the day after the coin went missing. He was wearing a uniform, one similar to those the custodians wear. Do you think he planted Dr. Langer's necklace in there?"

Joy lifted her hands and shrugged.

"Are you interested in coming with me to talk to him?" Evelyn asked.

"Sure." Joy smiled. "This is starting to get fun."

Fun wasn't quite the word Evelyn would use to describe how it felt—but she was starting to believe they were getting closer and closer to the answer.

Besides, she had no choice. The grand opening was just over a week away.

The basement of the Angel Wing was louder than usual as Evelyn and Joy entered about thirty minutes later. Steam hissed from the boilers, and the humidity from the dryers was thick. Employees pushed large canvas carts into the laundry room and exited with freshly folded sheets, blankets, and towels.

"I have never been down here," Joy said as her gaze swept over the massive space. "I've always wondered if they do laundry around the clock."

"I believe they do," Evelyn said. "I can't imagine how much work it is to keep all the linens fresh and clean."

The smell of bleach and other disinfectant cleaners was potent, stinging Evelyn's eyes as she led Joy through the basement to the custodial office.

Evelyn pushed open the door and was surprised to find the room empty.

"Maybe they're out to lunch," Joy said as she looked around the room. "It's like a whole new world down here. I often think the doctors and nurses are the backbone of this institution, but they couldn't do their job without the cleaning staff, could they?"

"Each department is important," Evelyn agreed. "We all need to do our jobs—everything from the cleaning staff to the food service to the security."

"And Records."

"And the gift shop." Evelyn smiled and then let out a sigh. "Looks like we'll need to come back to talk to Oscar."

"Which one is his desk?" Joy asked.

Evelyn walked down the row to the desk Oscar had been sitting at the last two times she was in the office. "He's usually right here."

His computer screen was black, and his desk was full of scraps of notepaper, a small stack of used, disposable coffee cups, and other office supplies.

"For being a custodian, he's not the most organized person," Joy mused.

Evelyn smiled and was about to turn away when she saw a check, partially tucked into an envelope. She wouldn't have thought to reach for it, except she saw the name *Dr. Sarah Langer* on the top, left-hand corner.

"Joy," Evelyn said, pointing at the check as she slowly lifted the envelope flap. "Look."

The check was written out to Oscar Maverick for five hundred dollars, and it was dated just yesterday. The envelope had the Charleston Museum logo with Mercy Hospital's address, in care of Oscar Maverick.

Joy's mouth dropped open. "Why would Dr. Langer write out a check to Oscar?"

"There's no note on the memo line." Evelyn bit her bottom lip and let the envelope close again. She couldn't think of a reason Dr. Langer might give Oscar money. It didn't line up with her earlier story. If she had turned down his advances, what possible reason could she have to pay him? She said he might try to frame her for a crime, but would that induce her to give him money? Was this blackmail, maybe? But for what? Did Oscar know something about Dr. Langer that she didn't want others to learn?

"What are you doing in here?" A man's voice reached Evelyn and Joy from the doorway.

Evelyn turned to find Oscar standing over the threshold, a scowl on his face. He was wearing a pair of jeans and a blue short-sleeved shirt. His name was embroidered on the right-hand side, though he also wore a hospital badge.

Taking a step away from his desk, Evelyn tried to offer him a smile. "We came to find you."

Oscar walked across the office while Evelyn and Joy backed away even farther. He looked down to see what they had been examining and quickly shoved the envelope under a stack of papers. "What do you want? Haven't you caused enough trouble?"

"Trouble?" Evelyn frowned, truly perplexed. "What trouble have I caused?"

"This hospital is in an uproar over that museum, and you're the one responsible."

Evelyn wasn't sure what he meant, since most people she knew were excited about the museum. Was he trying to employ a distraction so she wouldn't notice the check?

"I was wondering if we could ask you a few questions," Evelyn said as she motioned to Joy.

Oscar remained next to his desk as he stared at them. "What kind of questions?"

"Nothing too serious," Joy said with a chuckle. Evelyn appreciated that she was trying to lighten the mood.

"My niece mentioned that she saw someone near the tunnel opening the other night. Someone who fit your description."

"She saw me?" Oscar asked, his frown deepening.

Evelyn didn't answer, hoping he'd admit the truth on his own.

"Yeah? So? I work all sorts of hours, doing all sorts of jobs. I'm all over this campus."

"Isn't strange that you were near the tunnel opening the day after the coin was taken—in the middle of the night?"

Oscar shrugged.

"And when I came here to ask about the tunnel," Evelyn continued, "you didn't offer to tell Earl or me that you were there that night."

"I don't know anyone who tells the complete truth all the time. That's human nature."

Evelyn glanced at Joy, wondering what Earl would think if he heard Oscar saying these things.

"You're taking up my time," Oscar said. "I have better things to do."

"I have one more question." Evelyn wanted to know his real connection to Sarah Langer.

Oscar's jaw clenched as he leaned against his desk, irritation rolling off him in waves.

"Do you know a woman named Sarah Langer?"

The silence that followed Evelyn's question was thick. Oscar's face blanched, and he didn't speak.

"We believe you do know her," Joy said. "Quite well."

"What did she tell you?" Oscar asked. "More lies?"

"Lies?" Evelyn raised her brows.

"I don't care what she said." Oscar shoved away from his desk and ran his hand through his hair. "It wasn't my idea. She's the one who thought it would be easy, but it hasn't been, has it?"

"What hasn't been easy?" Evelyn frowned, not sure what he was talking about.

He paused and studied Evelyn. "She didn't tell you, did she?"

Evelyn didn't know what to say, so she shrugged. "She told me some interesting details about your relationship."

"Like how she won't leave me alone? How she calls me a dozen times a day and won't take no for an answer?"

Joy met Evelyn's gaze, questions filling her eyes. "Why is she calling you that often?"

"She's been stalking me is what it is," Oscar said, nodding his head as if he liked this new idea. "And I'm all but engaged to be married. My girlfriend isn't too happy about Sarah pestering me. I told her I'd be going to the police if she didn't stop bothering me." He nodded down at his desk. "That's why she paid me too. Told me she'd give me money if I kept my mouth shut. Doesn't want the embarrassment of people knowing what she's done."

"But she keeps calling and bothering you?" Evelyn asked. "Is she going to continue paying you so she can keep calling you?" The idea was a little absurd.

"Yeah." Oscar nodded.

"How did you meet her?" Joy asked.

"A bar."

"Recently?"

"Sure. About a month ago."

That did not line up with Dr. Langer's story at all. She claimed they'd known each other since childhood. Either one of them was lying, or both were.

"And this girlfriend," Evelyn said, "does she have a name? Might she know where you were the night the coin was taken from the museum?"

Oscar's reaction was swift as his anger reared up. "Where I was the night the coin was taken? Are you accusing me of stealing it?"

"You're the only person we know who was messing around the tunnel around the time the coin was taken, so you've become one of our prime suspects. But"—Evelyn shrugged—"if your girlfriend can offer you an alibi, you have nothing to worry about."

"I already know I have nothing to worry about," Oscar said with a tight mouth, "because I didn't take that coin, and you can't prove I did."

"Well," Evelyn admitted, "you might be right, but everything eventually comes to light. If you took it, we'll figure it out. Might be best to just return it tonight—that is, if you still have it." She held her breath. She sounded confident, but her heart felt like it was about to fail.

"You don't know what you're talking about," Oscar said, shaking his head. "And I don't know nothing about nothing. Now, if you don't have anything else to throw at me, you should get out. I have work to do."

Evelyn exhaled the breath she'd been holding. She motioned for Joy to follow her out of the custodial department, but it wasn't until they were in the relative privacy of the stairwell that she said, "What do you think of all that?"

"He's hiding something." Joy stopped on the stairs, her hand on the rail. "And something's fishy between him and Sarah Langer. Their stories are similar enough that it feels like they tried to corroborate—but one of them clearly missed the mark. And what about the check?"

"I agree. But where do we go from here?"

"I think you need to contact the police and let them know about the necklace and Shelby's account of seeing someone outside the tunnel entrance who matches Oscar's description. Maybe they can question Sarah and Oscar and get the truth out of them."

"Maybe you're right. I feel like all I've done is poke a sleeping bear. At least there's another plausible explanation for the coin missing. The tunnel opens a lot of possibilities."

They started up the stairs again, and Joy waved at Evelyn as she took a turn and went to the gift shop.

Evelyn felt like she'd hit another brick wall. Yet if she'd learned anything these past couple of weeks, it was that appearances weren't all that they seemed. And a brick wall might very well lead to a secret passageway.

Chapter Seventeen

THE WEEKEND HAD FINALLY COME, and with it, a chance for Evelyn to put aside her concerns and problems at work. It wasn't easy, since the coin was still missing, and Mr. Lorenzo had called, yet again, to see if anything had been discovered. She told him that she had contacted the police to tell them what she learned about Oscar and Sarah, but he wasn't impressed. Mr. Lorenzo was getting more and more impatient and upset, though Evelyn had tried to reassure him that she was doing everything she could to find the coin.

All day Saturday, Evelyn and James had spent time with Shelby, acting like tourists in their own hometown. They went out to Fort Sumter National Monument, taking a boat to see the famous location where the Civil War began. Afterward, they went into Charleston City Market to do a little shopping and eat lunch from one of the many food vendors. When they were full, they took a horse-drawn carriage ride around the historic district. They ended their day in White Point Garden after eating at Fleet Landing Restaurant for supper.

The day was everything Evelyn had hoped it would be. Shelby came alive again, her mood and attitude more joyful. Not once did she roll her eyes or shrug her shoulders with attitude. And not once did Evelyn mention the coin, Eric and Wanda's divorce, or the impending move to California. All James and Evelyn wanted was for Shelby to be carefree and happy—even if just for the day.

"Thank you for taking me around Charleston today," Shelby said to Evelyn and James as they sat on a bench overlooking Charleston Harbor. The sun was setting, casting brilliant colors across the sky.

"It was our pleasure," Evelyn said. "Did you see and do everything you wanted?"

Shelby smiled. "Everything but get an ice cream cone."

"The day's not done yet," James said with a chuckle. "I think ice cream sounds just about perfect. We should get some on our way home."

White Point Garden sat at the tip of the Charleston peninsula. It was a popular park with walking trails, shade trees, and lush carpets of grass. The historic mansions lining South Battery Street gave the park an almost storybook quality, adding to the charm and nostalgia.

Evelyn sat between Shelby and James. Her heart felt full and happy, even with the looming problems facing her next week if they didn't find the coin. She finally felt like she had broken through Shelby's hard exterior, getting a glimpse of the beautiful and kind heart within.

"I love you, Aunt Evelyn." Shelby hugged her without warning, resting her cheek against her shoulder.

Surprised tears sprang to Evelyn's eyes as she placed her hand on Shelby's forearm. Evelyn glanced at James, who couldn't hide his grin. He winked at her, the twinkle in his eyes saying, *I told you so.*

Maybe things would be okay for Shelby. With Rodney out of the picture, maybe she would have the courage to make a change for the better, despite her parents' divorce and despite her move across the country.

"I love you too, Shelbs," Evelyn said. "Promise me that even after you move to California, you'll come back and visit me often."

Shelby pulled away, but her smile was still lighting her eyes. "I love this city more than any other place on earth. When I'm old enough, I'm going to come back here."

"You can always go to college here," James said. "I know a pretty great university with the world's best history department."

"Actually," Shelby said, "I think that sounds like a great idea."

"Here's the thing." Evelyn met Shelby's gaze. "You have one year left of high school, and it's going to be one of the most important, especially because you're changing schools. If you want to go to college in Charleston, you'll need to keep your head down and focus on your schoolwork."

"Nobody can do it for you," James added. "Only *you* get to decide what kind of a future you're going to have, no matter what your parents have chosen for you up until this point. Every decision matters. The people you hang out with, where you work, your words and actions, and especially your treatment of others. Your future begins today."

Shelby laid her head on Evelyn's shoulder again as she looked at the harbor. "I wish I didn't have to go to California, but it's kind of exciting to think about starting over. No one knows me there, and the decisions I've made in Jacksonville won't change people's opinions about me. They'll only know the version of me I choose to show them."

"And," Evelyn said, placing her hand on Shelby's cheek, "if you show them the real you, they'll love you."

Shelby placed her hand over Evelyn's and gave it a slight squeeze. "Thank you, for everything."

"We're so happy you're here with us," Evelyn said.

"So am I."

James took Evelyn's free hand.

The sun slowly set, leaving the park in deep shadows.

"How about we go get that ice cream?" James asked. "Then we should head home and watch an old movie. Your choice, Shelby."

She lifted her head and grinned. "Do you still have *Bringing Up Baby* on DVD? I remember watching that last time I was here."

"Sure do," he said.

Shelby jumped off the bench and motioned for them to hurry up.

Evelyn's heart swelled with joy.

On Sunday, Shelby went to church with James and Evelyn. She was up before them and made their coffee and Evelyn's oatmeal before they even came downstairs. The change in Shelby was so drastic and had happened so quickly, Evelyn felt like she was spinning a bit. It was almost too good to be true, as if Shelby was being extra nice to cover up for something. Evelyn didn't want to think negatively about her niece and wanted to give her the benefit of the doubt, but it was still a little strange.

That evening, Evelyn, James, and Shelby walked toward the Mills House, an upscale restaurant and hotel in the historic district. Evelyn tried to push aside her doubts and misgivings about Shelby and enjoy the outing.

"The Mills House is one of my favorite restaurants in Charleston," Evelyn said to Shelby as they walked down Queen Street. It was only a ten-minute walk, which Evelyn appreciated, because she had dressed up for the occasion. She didn't wear heels often, but had chosen a black and white summer dress with a pair of black heels and a black shawl. Her silver hair was turned up in a small twist at the back. James was wearing a black suit, and Shelby had put on a simple black dress she had borrowed from Evelyn.

"It's not every day that a couple celebrates their thirty-fifth wedding anniversary," James said. "It's fun to go to a nice restaurant every once in a while, especially when we live in a city that's full of them."

"Is your actual anniversary today?" Shelby asked.

"It's tomorrow," Evelyn conceded, "but when Anne asked if we wanted to do something special to mark the occasion, this night worked better for her, Joy, and Shirley."

"Happy early anniversary," Shelby said.

Evelyn smiled, allowing herself to get lost in this moment.

The Mills House was a seven-story hotel in the heart of the historic district, across Meeting Street from Charleston City Offices. It was a soft pink in color with an ornate black balcony off the front on the second floor. One of its impressive features was a charming courtyard with a beautiful fountain in the center. As Evelyn, James, and Shelby turned from Queen Street and took a right onto Meeting Street, they passed the front of the building and headed toward the courtyard, where Anne told them to meet. They had to pass under an archway, which framed the fountain perfectly.

Evening had set, though there was a hint of light in the sky. Landscape lighting and candles on each of the wrought iron tables added a soft ambiance to the space. The sound of the water fountain was mellow and calming.

"Surprise!" A chorus of voices lifted in the air, making Evelyn jump and reach for James's hand.

A crowd of familiar faces smiled at James and Evelyn, the look of joy and delight shining from their eyes. Not only were Joy, Shirley, Anne, and Ralph there, but so were dozens of other people they knew. People from both Evelyn's and James's work, their neighbors, members from church, and even James's sister, Sylvia, from Myrtle Beach.

"What in the world?" Evelyn asked, her mouth dropping open in pure surprise and happiness.

Anne, Shirley, and Joy came and engulfed her in hugs.

"Happy anniversary," Joy said.

"Did the three of you plan this?" Evelyn asked.

"Guilty as charged." Shirley laughed as Garrison came up to her side. "Thirty-five years of marriage is something that should be celebrated big time."

Everyone was dressed in their very best, and waiters in black pants, white shirts, and long black aprons were mingling with the guests, offering platters of appetizers and beverages.

"This is too much," Evelyn said. "How can I ever repay you?"

"Hush," Anne said. She was wearing a pretty floral dress and a soft scarf. "This is our gift to you. Everyone pitched in, so don't worry about the bill. We want you to relax and enjoy yourself tonight."

"Leave everything at the door." Joy smiled. She was wearing a black dress with a soft pink cardigan and a beautiful pin at her shoulder. "Tonight, you're among friends and family, all here to make sure you and James know how much you're loved."

"Thank you." Evelyn looked at each of her friends. "I'm so blessed."

"Go and visit with your guests," Shirley said to her. "Everyone is eager to hear the secret to your happy marriage."

"Do you have a secret?" Shelby asked Evelyn, close to her elbow.

There were no other teenagers present, but Shelby didn't seem to mind. She looked up at Evelyn, expectation in her gaze.

"If I were to sum up what I think is the secret to a good marriage," Evelyn said, putting her arm around her niece, "it would be trust, communication, and always believing the best in your spouse—no matter how much they frustrate you."

Anne, Joy, and Shirley all chuckled, but Shelby just studied Evelyn, as if she was truly trying to take her advice to heart.

Evelyn and James mingled with their friends, enjoying the heavy appetizer party. With a celebration so different from their usual, day-to-day lifestyle, Evelyn felt very special. It was an anniversary party that she would not soon forget.

James held her hand as they mingled, staying close to her side. Shelby visited with Anne, Shirley, and Joy, and then pulled out her phone while the evening wore on.

Conversation and laughter flowed easily as people found seats at the tables or stood near the fountain.

Evelyn was glancing around the courtyard, trying to take in the moment, when she noticed two familiar faces.

"Will you excuse me?" Evelyn asked James and the couple they were visiting with.

"Of course," James said with a smile.

Evelyn moved across the space, smiling at people she knew and loved. Eventually, she made it to the table in the corner.

"Hello," Evelyn said to Stacia and Adam. They were leaning toward each other, their uneaten plates of food in front of them. Stacia was easily the most stylish person at the party with a slim black dress and tall black heels.

"Oh! There you are." Stacia stood and wrapped Evelyn in a tight hug. "Congratulations on thirty-five years of marriage. I have no idea how you do it."

Adam also stood, looking a little pleased with himself, no doubt because he was talking to Stacia—finally.

"Yeah," Adam said. "Congratulations. I haven't met your husband yet, and I wasn't sure if you'd want me to be here—"

"But when I asked him to come," Stacia said, "he couldn't say no."

Adam's cheeks filled with color, and he dipped his head in embarrassment.

Evelyn grinned, trying to hide her pleasure at the fact that the two of them had finally connected—and it had taken Stacia reaching out to Adam.

"Of course I'm happy you're here," Evelyn said. "I'd love to introduce you to my husband. He's heard so much about you over the past couple of months. He's the dean of the history department at the College of Charleston and has taken a special interest in our museum."

"Really?" Adam looked truly surprised. "I didn't know that."

"We both love history." Evelyn motioned for Adam and Stacia to follow her over to James. "He was the one who encouraged me to pursue the hospital museum idea."

When they arrived, James turned his full attention to Evelyn, Stacia, and Adam.

Evelyn quickly made the introductions, and after they had shaken hands, Adam said, "I'm sure Evelyn has told you all about the missing coin."

A niggle of unease settled in Evelyn's stomach as James looked at her. She had been trying to forget about it for just this one night, but it seemed to follow her everywhere she went.

"Yes, I've heard quite a lot about it," James said. "But I have a feeling Evelyn has put it out of her mind tonight to enjoy the party."

Evelyn smiled at his effort to redirect the conversation. He knew her so well.

"I wish I could forget about it," Adam said. "We have less than a week of work left before we're all done and can hand the museum over to the public. It's a shame the coin display will be empty."

"I have faith we'll find it in time," Evelyn said, pushing herself to smile.

"I hope you're right."

As Stacia and Adam walked away, James put his arm around Evelyn. "We won't give up hope," he said.

She forced herself to believe what he said, but when she caught a glance of Shelby, who had been watching their exchange with Stacia and Adam, Shelby's expression was hard to read. It almost looked like she was jealous.

Chapter Eighteen

THE PARTY LASTED LONGER THAN Evelyn expected, but even though it was a work night, she wasn't worried about the late hour. As they walked home under the bright moon, Evelyn took James's hand and let out a long, happy sigh.

"Did you enjoy yourself?" he asked her.

"More than you can imagine."

"Good." He smiled, and Evelyn knew that when she was happy, it made him happy.

Shelby walked on the other side of Evelyn, behind her just a bit. She had become quiet as the night progressed, with a marked difference in her mood after Evelyn and James spoke to Stacia and Adam.

"What about you?" Evelyn asked Shelby as she glanced back. "I'm sorry if it was boring for you to hang out with so many adults."

"I'm practically an adult," Shelby said, a bit defensively. "Not much younger than Stacia, anyway."

Stacia had graduated college the previous year, which made her about twenty-three.

"Six years is more of an age difference than you realize," Evelyn said. "Especially at this stage in your life. When you're as old as James and me, six years doesn't matter as much."

Shelby was quiet for a moment, and then said, "How old do you think Adam is?"

Evelyn thought for a moment. "He's been working with the South Carolina Historical Society for eight years, I believe he said. And, if my memory serves me correctly, I think he said he landed the job right out of college. He earned his master's degree while working at the historical society and is now the exhibit's program manager. I imagine he's about thirty—at the youngest."

"Thirty?" Shelby's eyes opened wide. "I didn't realize he was *that* old."

Evelyn smiled to herself, thinking about how young thirty felt to her now. But Adam was almost twice Shelby's age.

"What's this interest in Adam?" James asked.

Shelby shrugged as she looked down at her feet, a hint of color lighting her cheeks. "Nothing."

Did Shelby have a little crush on Adam? She had seemed to take a special interest in him the day she was at the hospital museum. Even though she asked the other team members a lot of questions, Adam was the one she focused most of her attention on. Was that why she got quiet during the party? Because she noticed Adam and Stacia together? It was clear the two of them were very interested in each other.

Evelyn cast James a knowing glance, and he winked at her.

When they arrived home Shelby said good night and went up to get ready for bed.

James and Evelyn stayed in the kitchen for a moment, enjoying a bit of the quiet they were so accustomed to.

"This was a very special night," James said as he took Evelyn into his arms. "Do you remember what we were doing thirty-five-years ago today?"

"After we had our rehearsal at church, we went to the restaurant and had our groom's dinner."

"And what about after that?" he asked.

Evelyn frowned as she looked up at him. "Nothing. I went home with my parents, and you went to your apartment."

He gave her a kiss and then whispered, "We said good night to each other, and for the last time, we went our separate ways to go to sleep. You to your home and me to mine. All I could think about that night was that I would never have to sleep alone again." He grinned. "I'm so thankful for thirty-five-years together. We've had our ups and downs, but through it all, I knew that we could always depend on each other. Thank you for that and so much more, Evie."

She hugged him tight and then took his hand and led him out of the kitchen, turning off the lights as she went.

Clouds filled the sky outside, covering the moon and the stars. Evelyn picked her way up the dark stairs, James following.

A crack of light from Shelby's bathroom shone in the dark hallway. A second later, she stepped into the corridor wearing her pajamas and a pair of slippers. "Good night," she called to them again before yawning and stepping into her bedroom.

"It's been nice seeing this new side of Shelby," James said as they walked into their own room. He flipped on the light, sat on the edge of the bed, and took off one of his shoes.

"I wouldn't call it new. It's nice to see the *old* Shelby."

He chuckled as he took off his second shoe. "I guess you're right."

Evelyn went to their bureau and removed her earrings to put into her jewelry box, which sat on top. She paused, almost afraid to bring up the subject. "But doesn't it feel strange—this sudden change in her whole demeanor and attitude? It's like she flipped a switch and, boom, she's the old Shelby again. Does that really happen? She was so angry and rude just a few days ago. I'm not trying to borrow trouble, but do you think it's authentic?"

James sighed as he stood and walked into their closet. "It sounds to me like you *are* trying to borrow trouble. People are capable of changing, Evie, even teenagers."

"I know." Evelyn took off her necklace and hung it on the hook in her case. "Why can't I just relax and enjoy myself? I just told Shelby tonight that the secret to a happy marriage is to always believe the best in your spouse—shouldn't that apply to everyone?"

James spoke to her from their closest. "Don't be so hard on yourself. Most of us know the good we should do, but we struggle to do it. Isn't that what the Apostle Paul said? In theory, and in practice, believing the best is always the right policy. But in reality, sometimes that gets us into trouble." He left the closet wearing his pajama bottoms and a white T-shirt. "But we've forgiven Shelby, and we're going to believe the best about her. Even if she messes up again—which, since she's human, she will—we'll continue to believe in her. Over and over again, for as long as it takes."

Evelyn smiled. "You're too good for me."

"That's funny. I always thought it was the other way around." He gave her a quick kiss before entering their bathroom to brush his teeth.

After they were in bed Evelyn lay there for a long time in the dark—much longer than she should have with work in the morning—and relived several moments from that evening at the Mills House. The surprise, the joy, and the pleasure she had taken from being with everyone filled her to the brim.

James began to snore softly, and Evelyn turned to her side to look out the window. It was completely dark, with only a hint of color from a streetlight on the end of the road, behind the neighbor's house.

Wind picked up, rattling the windows and gusting against the eaves. A shiver ran down Evelyn's spine, though she wasn't cold. Something wasn't right, though she couldn't put her finger on it. Was it Shelby? Was it the museum? The party? Her friends?

She chastised herself for her wild imagination and tried to go to sleep.

The wind continued to blow, and Evelyn forced herself to keep her eyes closed. She lay there for what felt like an hour when she started to finally drift off to sleep—

A noise made her open her eyes. It was more than the wind and more than the normal settling of the house.

It sounded like someone had bumped into a piece of furniture downstairs.

Shelby?

Evelyn sat up and glanced at James's side of the bed. He was still there, sleeping soundly. He had an early morning, and she didn't want to bother him, especially if it was only Shelby bumping around in the night.

But why would she be moving around downstairs?

A new thought made Evelyn move a little faster. What if Shelby was sneaking out again?

A knot formed in Evelyn's chest. She wanted to trust Shelby like James suggested, but at what cost? She wouldn't let Shelby play them for fools—again.

Evelyn stepped into her slippers and pulled a robe from the foot of her bed. She tiptoed out of her bedroom and walked down the hall to Shelby's room. Without even knocking or telling her she was coming in, Evelyn pushed open Shelby's door.

But Shelby was lying on her bed, clearly sleeping. She wore a headband to keep her hair off her face, and she had one of those white pimple pads on her nose. It was obvious she wasn't going anywhere anytime soon—and probably hadn't been downstairs either.

So what had Evelyn heard? Was it just the wind? Was it her imagination?

She slowly closed Shelby's door and decided to go downstairs to check and make sure something wasn't causing the noise.

As she walked from one room to the next, nothing looked out of place or suspicious.

Maybe the wind had caused a piece of siding or roof to blow off and create the sound.

Evelyn walked back up the stairs, pulling her robe tighter around her waist. Her imagination was strong tonight, that was for sure. In the morning, she would have a good laugh about it with James.

With that thought in mind, Evelyn went back to bed and fell into a deep, restful sleep.

The morning sunshine spread across Evelyn's face. She blinked several times as she tried to wake herself up.

"Morning, sleepyhead," James said. He leaned down and kissed Evelyn's cheek. "Happy anniversary."

Evelyn turned to her husband and wrapped her arms around his neck. "Happy anniversary," she said.

"I wish I didn't have to go to work." He sat on the bed next to her, dressed for the day. "Maybe we should both play hooky and run away together."

"Wouldn't that be nice?" Evelyn ran her hands over her face, rubbing it gently. "I wish I could, but we're only five days away from the museum's grand opening, and I have so much to do. I have to place the final order for the appetizers today, and the *Charleston Times* is stopping by to take some pictures and interview Adam and me for a feature article."

"Ah, the joys and responsibilities of adulthood." James chuckled. "How about I stop somewhere and pick up supper for tonight? One less thing for you to worry about."

Evelyn smiled. "What will you pick up?"

"It'll be a surprise." He kissed her again, his beard tickling her cheek, and then rose from the bed. "I need to get on the road if I'm going to be on time this morning."

"Have a good day," Evelyn said as she sat up and stretched.

James left their bedroom, and Evelyn got out of bed. She grabbed her clothes from the spot where she laid them out the night before and went into the bathroom to get ready for the day.

The front doorbell rang, causing Evelyn to frown. Who would be at their house so early? She wasn't expecting a package to be delivered, or a service technician, or anything else that would make someone stop by this morning.

James would still be downstairs making his coffee and would answer. Out of curiosity, Evelyn put on her robe and slippers and went to their bedroom door to listen.

It was impossible for Evelyn to hear what was being said from where she was standing, so she moved to the top of the stairway. Even there, it wasn't easy, but at least she could make out a few words.

"Can I help you?" James asked, concern tightening his voice.

"Is this the home of Evelyn Ruth Perry?"

"Yes." Again, it was the concern in James's voice that made Evelyn's anxiety rise. "Is there a problem?"

"We have a court-ordered search warrant to inspect the premises," the man said.

Evelyn's eyes grew wide, and her heart started to pound. Who was James talking to?

"Evelyn!" James called out to her.

She was already on the stairs, making her way toward the downstairs hallway. She didn't care that she was in her bathrobe and slippers or that her hair was probably sticking out in every conceivable direction. She didn't even care that she hadn't brushed her teeth yet or that she needed her morning shower.

When she saw the two police officers standing at her front door, a search warrant in hand, Evelyn didn't notice anything other than their grim faces.

"Are you Evelyn Ruth Perry?" the taller officer asked.

Evelyn swallowed and nodded. "I am."

"We have a search warrant here to inspect your property."

"A search warrant for what?" Evelyn grasped the lapels of her robe as she stood close to James. He put his arm around her, drawing her close to offer his support.

"We have reason to believe that the twenty-dollar gold coin taken from the Mercy Hospital Museum is somewhere on your property."

Evelyn's mouth fell open, and she just stared at the two police officers.

"Do you offer your consent for us to search this property?" the taller officer, whose name badge said P. STANDISH, asked.

Evelyn's mouth was dry as she looked to James, having no idea what rights, if any, they had in this situation. James simply nodded once, his clear blue eyes filled with concern, yet confidence.

"Yes," Evelyn croaked out. "Yes, of course. But you won't find the coin here."

The two officers entered the house and immediately went into the dining room to begin their search.

James and Evelyn stayed in the hallway, near the front door.

"What's happening?" Evelyn asked James. "How did they get a search warrant, and why would they think the coin is here?"

"Search warrants are issued by judges when the police bring affidavits to court." James kept one eye on the police officers as he spoke to Evelyn. "Either the police in charge of the investigation or someone connected gave statements, taken under oath, to offer probable cause. Someone must believe that you have the coin, and the police had to make a valid case before a judge to get this search warrant."

"But who would do something like that?" Evelyn asked. "I proved that I wasn't the last person to see the coin."

"You didn't prove anything, Evie. You offered an alternative explanation, but it proved nothing." He looked at her closely. "Who do you think did this?"

"The only person I can think of would be Mr. Lorenzo, the director at the conservation center. He's been suspicious of me from the start, and he's losing patience. But this is all pointless." Evelyn's hands hurt from how hard she was clutching her robe lapels. "They won't find anything. I have no idea where the coin is. If I did, I would have brought it to everyone's attention."

"Unfortunately, Mr. Lorenzo must not believe you." James's face began to soften. "But you're right. We have nothing to worry about. The coin's not here, so this is just a waste of time."

The police worked quickly and efficiently as they went through the sideboard and hutch.

"You're going to be late for work," Evelyn said to James as the police moved into the kitchen. "This could take hours."

"I'm not leaving your side." James pulled his cell phone out of his pocket. "I'll text Dr. Henderson and let him know I won't be at work this morning."

"I'm sorry," Evelyn said.

"It's not your fault, Evie."

"What a great way to spend our anniversary." The sarcasm dripped from Evelyn's voice.

James smiled. "It's memorable, that's for sure."

The sunshine continued to pour into the house, warming Evelyn as she stood near the window and watched the police go through her entire kitchen from top to bottom. She wanted to get dressed, but she didn't want to leave their sight—and wasn't even sure if she could.

As they moved to the living room, James finally said to Evelyn, "Go get dressed. I'll keep watch."

"Are you sure?"

"Of course. And make sure Shelby wakes up. The officers will probably move upstairs next, and we don't want her to be awakened by police officers entering her bedroom."

"Good thinking." Evelyn sped up the stairs, planning to wake Shelby and then get dressed as quickly as possible.

Shelby was just leaving her bedroom, scratching her head, as Evelyn arrived at the top of the stairs.

"Good morning." Shelby blinked a couple of times. "Aren't you usually dressed by now?"

"There are police officers downstairs with a search warrant."

Shelby's eyes instantly became alert. "Why?"

"Someone thinks the gold coin is here and offered enough probable cause for a judge to grant a search warrant."

"Probable cause?" Shelby frowned. "What kind?"

"I don't know, but it must have been convincing. James is downstairs with the police right now. They're looking through the living room but will probably move up here next."

Evelyn didn't wait to discuss the situation further. She went into her bedroom and quickly threw on a pair of slacks and a blouse. She brushed her hair and teeth. She'd have to shower later. Right now, she needed to get back downstairs.

She was just leaving the bedroom again when James came up the stairway and into the hallway, his face filled with the most awful look of dread Evelyn had ever seen in her life.

Her heart fell at the sight, and she instantly became weak. "Did they find it?"

He swallowed, his face ashen. "In the curio cabinet, in the living room."

"*What?*" Evelyn leaned against the doorframe, her body weak. "How is that possible?"

"I don't know. But I saw them find it myself. They opened the cabinet, and there it was—as plain as day."

"I don't understand. How did it get there?"

Shelby's bedroom door opened at that moment. She glanced up and met their gazes, and in an instant, her entire demeanor changed. "They found it?"

The way she said it—as if she knew they would—made something snap inside Evelyn.

"How could you do this to us?" Evelyn choked on the words. "I trusted you, and you betrayed me. I was afraid you took the coin all along—but I wanted to believe otherwise."

Shelby stood, motionless, as she stared at Evelyn but made no move to deny her claims.

"They want to talk to you," James said to Evelyn. He took her into his arms, and she could feel his heart pounding. "Because the coin is worth so much, they'll probably arrest you."

Nothing had prepared Evelyn for this moment. Never in her life had she anticipated being arrested—especially for something she didn't do. Why were they arresting her? What about Shelby—or even James? Any of them could have taken it, as far as the police were concerned. Did they have reason to believe it was her?

"What happens next?" she heard herself saying, though she felt like she was having an out-of-body experience. Her voice sounded so far away.

"I'll follow you to the station and call our lawyer on the way." James swallowed hard. "We'll get you out of there as fast as we can."

Evelyn moved to the stairway and caught a glimpse of Shelby out of the corner of her eye. She looked defeated and scared, not to mention extremely small and innocent—but Evelyn now knew she was capable of much bigger lies and crimes than she had first believed.

Chapter Nineteen

Evelyn had never been as humiliated or mortified as she was during the five hours it took for James to get her released her from the Charleston Police Department. The whole ordeal felt like it added a decade to her life, though everything went by in a blur—being placed in handcuffs, riding to the police department in the back of the squad car, and then waiting in a windowless holding cell. Eventually, they transferred her to the county courthouse, where a judge agreed to let her go on bail. But then Evelyn and James spent another hour with their lawyer, discussing the case.

"We have a little time," Constance Williamson said as she sat across from them in a conference room within the courthouse. The room was dressed with age. Thick trim work, heavy light fixtures, and dark furniture filled the space. "The prosecuting attorney will want ample time to make his case before we go before the judge again."

"How much time do we have?" James asked.

"Right now, the judge has set the court date for the end of next month, but I wouldn't be surprised if the prosecuting attorney asks for an extension."

Evelyn's head hurt, and her stomach was roiling. She'd never felt so ill in all her life. "I didn't take the coin. How can I prove my innocence?"

"Unfortunately, you were the last known person to see the coin, and it was found in your home." Constance shook her head. "Not to mention these sworn statements. It's going to be difficult to prove you didn't take it, though we'll do everything we can to put reasonable doubt in the jury's mind."

"This is such a nightmare." Evelyn looked to James, hoping and praying he would have the answers she needed. She hated that anyone would believe her capable of doing such a thing. "What are we going to do?"

He took her hand and squeezed it tight. "Whatever it takes."

"Can I at least know who gave the affidavits to the police?" Evelyn asked.

Constance opened the file she'd been given by the judge and flipped through a couple of pages before pulling out the affidavits. "There are two here. One is from a Dr. Sarah Langer, who claims she saw the coin in your possession when she was at your house."

"At my house?" Evelyn rose out of her chair, ready to fight someone. "Sarah Langer has never been in my house. It's a lie!"

"You need to calm down, Evelyn," Constance said. "I'm not the enemy here."

Evelyn's heart was beating so hard, she could hear it pulsing in her ears. She took several deep breaths as she resumed her seat. "I'm sorry."

"I understand you're upset." Constance was in her mid- to late forties and attended church with them. Her calm voice and brilliant mind were two of the reasons James had called on her. "But we're not going to win this thing by losing our cool, Evelyn. As hard as it is, we need to remain as unemotional as possible."

Evelyn swallowed and nodded. "Okay. I understand."

James slipped his hand to Evelyn's back and rubbed gently. "Who is the other affidavit from?"

Constance flipped to the next page and read for a couple of seconds before saying, "His name is Oscar Maverick. It looks like he's a custodian at Mercy Hospital. He claims he saw Evelyn exiting the underground tunnel at Mercy Hospital on the night the coin was taken."

"I can't believe it." Evelyn forced herself to remain calm, though she gripped the edge of the table until her knuckles turned white. "He was the one seen outside the tunnel."

"By Shelby," James added.

"And she's your niece?" Constance asked, writing Shelby's name on a legal pad.

"Yes," Evelyn said.

"And could she be the one responsible for all of this?"

Evelyn looked at James, studying his face, trying to lean into his strength. "I thought she was guilty, but now that I know who gave the sworn affidavits, I'm convinced it was Dr. Langer and Oscar who took the coin. There are a few other clues that point to their guilt."

"Not to mention that you called the diner where Shelby was eating with her boyfriend the night the coin went missing," James reminded her. "They gave Shelby an alibi."

Evelyn had forgotten that information in all the chaos that morning. She was ashamed that she had blamed Shelby again.

"Well," Constance said, "for now, you should probably go home and try to get some rest. You've been through a rough experience, and I want you to keep your mind sharp for the days and weeks ahead. We're going to need to prepare our case."

The very thought made Evelyn feel dizzy. She couldn't imagine enduring weeks of this—and then what? Prison? Panic and desperation gripped her chest. "What if I can prove it was Dr. Langer and Oscar?"

"And how would you do that?"

"I don't know." Evelyn looked down at the stack of papers in front of Constance. "But there has to be a way. Dr. Langer and Oscar know each other, though both of them gave different accounts of how they met. Oscar was seen near the tunnel entrance, yet he omitted that information when I asked him about it, and I found Dr. Langer's necklace in the passageway, which my friend, Shirley Bashore can corroborate. Then I discovered a check that Dr. Langer made out to Oscar for five hundred dollars. I know it was them."

"And whoever took the coin knew a thing or two about how to get into the display case," James added. "They didn't destroy anything and even took the time to replace the case top. Dr. Langer would have the expertise to get into the case."

"My advice to you," Constance said as she closed her file, "is to stay as far away from Dr. Langer and Mr. Maverick as you can. We will use the information you've just given me, but it could severely compromise our case if you try to do any more investigating."

Constance looked at her watch and then shoved her file into her briefcase. "I need to run, but I'll pencil in some time to meet with you in a couple of days. In the meantime, think about any other information that might help our case—and stay away from Dr. Langer and Mr. Maverick. If anything happens to either one of them, it won't look good in court."

Evelyn frowned. She would never physically harm them, but she couldn't promise Constance that she would leave this case alone. There had to be a way to prove that the pair was guilty. Evelyn couldn't sit back and let this go to court. Not only would it be humiliating, but it wouldn't be right—not when the real culprits were getting away with their plans.

"Thank you," James said to Constance as he reached out and shook her hand. "We appreciate you coming on such short notice."

"I'm happy to help." Constance shook Evelyn's hand too. "The coin is being returned to the conservation center. I heard that Mr. Lorenzo is very pleased to get it back."

"The only good thing that has come from this whole affair." Even as Evelyn said the words, she wished she could feel happy about the return of the coin.

Constance held the door open for them, and they entered the large central hall. People were walking up and down the tile floor, popping into and out of office doors. The courtroom was at the far end of the building. Evelyn hoped she never had to come here again.

They parted ways with Constance outside. The day was hot and humid, and the sun was blazing in a cloudless sky.

As James and Evelyn walked toward their car, James stopped on the sidewalk and turned to her. "There's one question neither of us has asked."

Evelyn paused. "What?"

"How did the coin get in our curio cabinet? I don't think Shelby did this—do you?"

A small wedding party went by. The bride was wearing a simple white dress with a short veil and carrying a small bouquet. There were only a few people with them, but they were all grinning. It was a stark reminder to Evelyn that today was her thirty-fifth wedding anniversary—though it was a day she wished she could forget forever.

"No," she finally answered James. "I don't think Shelby did this. I truly believe it's Dr. Langer and Oscar."

"But how did they get the coin into our house?"

Evelyn's eyes opened wide, and she put her hand on James's arm. "Last night something woke me up. I thought it was Shelby sneaking out again, but she was sound asleep. I walked through the house but didn't notice anything, so I went back to bed."

"You think someone broke in last night?"

"It's a possibility—unless they did it before last night. But I don't doubt that either Dr. Langer or Oscar planted the coin in our cabinet at some point."

"Why would they do it?" James asked. "What are their motives?"

"Anger, resentment, retaliation. Both of them were upset about the museum, for their own reasons."

"And you think they found each other and worked out this plan together?"

"I do." Evelyn started to walk toward their car again, and James followed. "The question is whether or not they originally thought to frame me for it. But now that I'm onto them, they had no other choice."

"What will we do about it?"

"I don't know—but I'm calling Joy, Anne, and Shirley. They'll help us come up with a plan." Evelyn was already pulling her phone out of her purse to text them.

If anyone could help Evelyn right now, it was her Mercy friends.

It was less than a five-minute drive from the Charleston County Courthouse to Evelyn's house. She hadn't eaten all day, but she couldn't even think about food right now. She'd never been so upset before, and she couldn't see the end. If she was convicted of this crime, she could be facing time in prison. The coin's value made the crime a felony, which meant a minimum of a year in a county or state prison. She couldn't even think about that right now or she might start to seriously panic.

"It's going to be okay," James said to Evelyn, taking her hand the moment he parked the car in their driveway. "We'll figure this out."

"What if we don't?"

"Don't even think such a thing." He squeezed her hand and got out of the car.

Evelyn followed. Though it had been less than six hours since she was arrested, it felt like she'd been away from home for years.

James unlocked the back door, and Evelyn entered the living room.

"Does the lock look tampered with?" she asked him.

"No." He closed the door. "I'll check around the house and see if anything looks out of place."

"I'm going to go find Shelby while I wait for the girls to get here."

Evelyn had told Anne, Joy, and Shirley what happened via text and asked them to come to her house. She called Stacia and briefly told her as well, though she asked that Stacia not mention it to anyone. Finally, Evelyn had called Garrison and told him all the details. He suggested she take the rest of the day off, and the remaining week, if she wanted. But she couldn't take off the week. There was too much to do—yet she knew this would be a public relations nightmare for Garrison if the information leaked, which meant they were working against the clock.

Evelyn and James went their separate ways. James to look at all the windows and doors, and Evelyn upstairs to find Shelby, since she wasn't on the main floor.

"Shelby?" Evelyn called out to her as she walked up the stairs.

No reply.

Entering her room, Evelyn tried to smile for Shelby's sake—but Shelby wasn't in her room either.

In fact, she was nowhere to be found in the house or in the courtyard.

Shelby was gone.

Evelyn went to her purse and pulled out her phone. She tried calling, but there was no answer. She texted her, hoping her niece would respond.

"James!" Evelyn said as she met him near the kitchen. "Shelby's not here."

"Did you try calling her?"

"Yes. Where do you think she went?"

"I don't know. Hopefully she just needed some time to herself. I'm sure she's upset."

"I don't like her being out there by herself."

"She's seventeen, and it's daylight." James put his hands on Evelyn's shoulders. "She'll be fine."

"But she was supposed to let me know when she goes out."

"You were a little preoccupied."

Evelyn forced herself to calm down. It wasn't surprising that everything was making her more upset than usual today.

"I found one of the windows in the living room cracked open," James said. "We must have forgotten to lock it, which means someone could have easily opened it last night and climbed in without doing any damage."

"That must be how they got in."

The front doorbell rang, and Evelyn jumped.

"It's probably the gals," James said as he laid his hand on her arm to calm her.

"You're right." Evelyn moved away from James and answered the door.

Sure enough, Anne, Joy, and Shirley all stood on the front stoop.

Anne's eyes were filled with horror as she rushed across the threshold and embraced Evelyn. "How are you? Are you hurt?"

"Hurt?" Evelyn returned her friend's hug and shook her head. "No. Just upset—and jumpy."

Joy and Shirley also hugged Evelyn as they came into the house.

Evelyn closed the door behind them. "Let's go to the living room where we can be comfortable."

They moved down the hall. As Evelyn passed the kitchen, she saw James putting a pot of coffee on. He smiled at her as they walked by.

She returned the smile, so thankful for his calm, steady presence.

As soon as the women were settled in the living room, Shirley jumped in with her first question. "Can you tell us exactly what happened?"

Evelyn relayed the whole story, including the strange sound that had awakened her the night before, the search, the arrest, and coming home to find Shelby gone and one of the windows cracked open. She realized it helped her process the experience as she shared it with her friends.

"I agree with you," Shirley said. "I think Dr. Langer and Oscar are to blame."

"They're the most likely suspects," Joy agreed. "I thought as much even before they gave false statements—under oath, no less."

"So," Anne said as she accepted the cup of coffee that James offered her, "the question remains. How do we get them to admit their guilt?"

James handed out the rest of the steaming cups he'd brought from the kitchen and took the seat next to Evelyn on the sofa. The coffee smelled delicious and made Evelyn's stomach growl with hunger for the first time that day.

"You think they'd actually admit their guilt?" James asked.

"Not to the authorities," Anne said. "But they might to Evelyn, if they think she's alone."

"It might be the only way to know for sure," Evelyn said. "There isn't a lot of evidence to convict them at this point. If we went to the authorities with the little that we have, it would look like we were retaliating. We need their confessions."

"Do you think we could actually get them to admit it?" Joy asked, leaning forward. "And, if so, how?"

"I don't know." Anne took a sip of her coffee as she stared straight ahead, apparently in thought. "If we could get them together and talking while we had the authorities nearby to overhear, then we could clear Evelyn's name."

"It's not a half-bad idea," Shirley said.

"Why, thank you." Anne lifted an eyebrow with mock offense.

A small smile tilted Evelyn's lips. She didn't feel so alone or so helpless with James and her friends nearby, trying to come up with a plan to help her.

"I doubt we could get Dr. Langer to the hospital," Joy said. "She probably wants to stay as far from there as possible."

"And I doubt we could get Oscar to the Charleston Museum," Evelyn said. "They're probably trying to keep a low profile."

"There has to be a time and a place they'd both come." Shirley set her cup on a coaster. "Do you think we could get Oscar into the museum for a cleaning or maintenance or something?"

"Adam and his team should be finishing up their work today." Evelyn wrapped her hands around her cup a little tighter. "He said he planned to have all their tools and equipment out of there by five." An idea started to form. "I could tell Dr. Langer that I'd like to talk to her about Blackbeard's medicine chest and I'd like to do it at the museum."

"Do you think she would come?" James asked.

"I think she'd do just about anything where the medicine chest is concerned." Evelyn's mind was already moving through the possible encounter. "At the same time, I could request a meeting with Oscar to talk to him about the specific duties I'd like the custodial staff to oversee once the museum opens."

"How would we hide the authorities?" Shirley asked.

Evelyn smiled. "We could have them waiting in the secret passageway. If the trapdoor is open, they shouldn't have any trouble hearing a conversation between us in the museum. I'll just make sure it takes place near the opening."

"Are you sure you want to go through with this plan?" James asked Evelyn. "Constance said we should stay as far away from Dr. Langer and Oscar as possible. If this works, and you can actually get them together, things might not go the way we hope. They might gang up on you and then the authorities would hear them corroborating each other's stories."

"It's a risk I have to take." Evelyn was willing to do just about anything to clear her name. "I need to try."

"If you're sure…"

"I'm very sure. But I don't think getting them to talk about what happened will be the problem. Coordinating a time when they'll both come to the museum, without the other knowing, will be the tricky part."

"And," Anne added, "we only have one chance. If they figure out what we're trying to do, they'll never agree to meet with you again."

"We need to pray," Shirley said. "Pray that God will orchestrate this event and that it will work to free Evelyn of the blame."

"Shall we pray now?" Joy asked.

"No time like the present." James set his cup on a coaster and moved forward on his seat.

The women followed, all of them bowing their heads.

As James prayed for Evelyn, she was filled with the most amazing sense of calm and assurance.

She just hoped and prayed that it would continue.

Chapter Twenty

IT HADN'T BEEN EASY, BUT Evelyn was able to arrange a meeting with both Oscar and Dr. Langer at five o'clock. Oscar was coming under the pretense to talk about Evelyn's custodial expectations, and Dr. Langer was coming to discuss Blackbeard's medicine chest. Neither one mentioned their part in the affidavits that had gotten Evelyn arrested, nor did Evelyn mention that the police had been to her house earlier that morning. When speaking to both Oscar and Dr. Langer, Evelyn had kept all of that information to herself.

Now, as she stood in the quiet museum, waiting for the pair to arrive, she forced herself to breathe deeply. She still hadn't heard from Shelby, but James said he'd keep trying to find her.

Evelyn inhaled, attempting to appreciate the accomplishments before her. The museum was finished—completed just as they had hoped, with a few days to spare before the official grand opening. Adam and his team had finalized the last of their work earlier than anticipated and had left around three.

What Oscar and Dr. Langer didn't know was that Seamus had a couple of police officers in the secret room right beneath the opening, recording their conversation.

The only thing not in place was the gold coin, which would probably not be returned to Mercy Hospital in time, even if Evelyn could prove she wasn't guilty of taking it.

Under different circumstances, Evelyn would be thrilled with the museum. But it was difficult to have any emotion right now other than anxiety. Her nerves were on end with the upcoming meeting but also the larger threat to her reputation. Not to mention the possibility of being charged for a crime she didn't commit.

"Evelyn?" Seamus climbed up the ladder from the room below. "Are you ready?"

She nodded, afraid her voice might not work properly if she tried to speak.

"Don't worry about us," Seamus said. "Just get them talking, and hopefully they'll say what we need to hear."

"Thank you," Evelyn said to Seamus. "I know you don't have to believe me and didn't have to come here."

He smiled at her, his blue eyes shining with admiration. "You've been nothing but kind and respectful these past few years. My experiences with Oscar are not so positive, and when push comes to shove, it's easier to believe he's behind this than you. But"—he paused and shrugged—"I need proof. A confession would be ideal."

"I understand." Evelyn swallowed the panic rising up her throat. What if she couldn't get them to confess? What if they were so upset about being tricked into the museum at the same time that they didn't say anything?

A movement at the door brought Evelyn's head up, and Seamus disappeared back into the hidden room.

Sarah Langer entered the museum, wearing a pencil skirt and a matching navy blue blazer. Her curly red hair was twisted up into a tight bun, and she carried a set of keys in one hand and a cell phone in the other. Her gaze swept over the museum, and if Evelyn wasn't mistaken, she saw a bit of surprise and approval in her eyes.

Evelyn stood still, wanting Dr. Langer to come to her, instead of the other way around.

"I'm impressed," Dr. Langer said. "This looks like real museum-quality work."

"Adam and his team were beyond professional." Evelyn lifted her chin, remembering that she wasn't the guilty party. She had nothing to be ashamed of or worried about—unless she couldn't get her to talk.

Dr. Langer walked over to Evelyn and glanced at the trapdoor. "What's this?"

"A secret tunnel we discovered during the installation process." Evelyn moved aside so the other woman could take a look, trusting that Seamus and the police officers were out of sight. "We're going to do some research to see if there's any historical significance to the hospital and perhaps turn it into an exhibit." Adam was already working on it. "We've determined that whoever took the coin must have used this secret passageway to get in and out of the museum."

"Hmm." Dr. Langer didn't comment one way or the other. But she did finally turn to Evelyn and say, "What's this about Blackbeard's chest? What did you want to discuss?"

The museum door opened again, saving Evelyn from needing to answer her question, and this time Oscar entered. He was wearing his usual jeans and blue work shirt. When he saw them, he paused, midstride.

"What are you doing here?" he asked Dr. Langer.

Her face betrayed nothing. "I've come to discuss something I want. What are you doing here?"

Oscar looked to Evelyn, a scowl forming on his face. "I thought I was here to meet with Evelyn about the museum, but I'm thinking she wanted me here for a different reason."

"I invited you here to talk about the museum," Evelyn said quickly. It was true—at least, in part. "Why don't you join us?"

Oscar looked around the museum, his gaze skeptical, before he approached them. He glanced at the trapdoor briefly but didn't say anything.

Dr. Langer crossed her arms. "What does Oscar have to do with Blackbeard's chest?"

"I wasn't sure at first," Evelyn said cautiously, not wanting to pounce too fast. "But I think I've figured it out."

Both of them watched her carefully, frowns on their faces. She felt bold, knowing Seamus and the police were nearby.

"I'm not sure how you two know each other," Evelyn said, "but I do know that you, Dr. Langer, were never happy about bringing the medicine chest back to Mercy. Perhaps you thought that if the museum seemed unsafe or if I was painted as incompetent, that Garrison would close it down and you would get the artifacts back for your own museum."

"They belong there," Dr. Langer said. "They've been a part of our collection for so long that it was a travesty to move them. It's not a secret that I thought you were incompetent from the start."

Evelyn chose to ignore her insult and continued. "Somehow, you two started to talk about the museum, and you devised a plan to use the secret passageway to get in and take something valuable. It couldn't be the medicine chest, since that was too obvious and would immediately point to you, so you took the only other thing that had widespread appeal and value. The gold coin." She looked at Dr. Langer. "And you paid Oscar five hundred dollars to complete this deed."

"How clever you are," Dr. Langer said to Evelyn. "Everything all wrapped up in a neat little bow."

"The question is whether or not you intended to frame me for the crime," Evelyn said.

"That was just a happy coincidence." She walked around Evelyn and touched the barricade surrounding the trapdoor. "I didn't even think about the fact that you were the only person to have a key and would be the last to leave."

Evelyn turned to face her, needing her to actually admit to the crime so the police could hear her.

"Did you do it alone?" she asked.

"Why do you think it was me?"

"Because I found your necklace in the tunnel."

"You don't think Oscar framed me, then?"

"Are we back to that?" Oscar asked. "Are you going to pin this on me when you were the one to come up with the plan?"

"You were the one to execute it," she said.

"And you were right beside me the whole time." Oscar approached her. "I have your check to prove it."

"Is that why you didn't cash it yet?" she asked him. "Just in case you needed proof that I paid you to take the coin?"

"Maybe." Oscar shrugged. "A man can never be too careful in a situation like this."

"Great." Dr. Langer's voice dripped with sarcasm. "But it's not going to come down to that, is it?" She smiled at Oscar and chuckled. "Pretty soon we won't have to worry about being charged with taking the coin."

He returned her laugh, and they both looked at Evelyn.

So they didn't know that the police had been at her house or that she had been arrested and released earlier that day. She could use that to her benefit.

"How do you think you'll get away with it?" Evelyn asked, weak with relief that they'd admitted to their guilt so easily. "That coin doesn't belong to you."

"Oh, it'll be returned to the conservation center," Dr. Langer said. "I never intended to harm it. Eventually it will go back where it belongs, after we've used it to secure our innocence."

"Where is it now?" Evelyn knew the answer but needed to keep them talking. They'd already said enough, but Evelyn wanted everything.

"It's right where it needs to be," Oscar said.

"You took the coin, and now you're going to use it for what purpose?" Evelyn looked between the pair of them.

"To get this museum closed down, of course," Dr. Langer said. "That was the plan all along."

"How?"

"The police are on their way to your house," she said, "probably as we speak. And they're going to find the coin right where we planted it. You'll go to prison, and the resulting embarrassment to the hospital will hopefully close this museum down. I'll get the chest back and everyone will be happy."

"You honestly think that would work?" Evelyn couldn't believe the woman was so naive. "All that will happen is that my life will be ruined. The museum won't close, and you won't get the medicine chest back."

"Well"—she lifted a shoulder—"it's worth a shot."

"I think we've heard enough." Seamus appeared at the ladder. He climbed up with the police close behind.

Dr. Langer and Oscar stepped back. The shock on their faces soon turned to anger.

"You set us up!" Dr. Langer said to Evelyn.

"No," Evelyn said with a heavy sigh. "You set me up. I was only proving my innocence."

"We heard everything," Seamus said. "There's no need to lie anymore or make this worse than it already is."

Dr. Langer's face turned ashen, and Oscar's face turned bright red with rage.

The relief that Evelyn felt was bittersweet. She hated to see the pair face prison, knowing their sentence would be even greater since they not only stole the coin but gave false statements under oath and tried to frame her. But, unlike Evelyn, they deserved their punishment.

And it meant that she was free.

"Evelyn!" Joy called out as Evelyn walked down the hall toward the main entrance, where James said he'd be waiting for her.

Joy, Shirley, and Anne all rose from their chairs. After leaving her house, they had come to the hospital together, but they had agreed it would be best if they didn't interfere in the museum. James had waited in the car, while Shirley, Anne, and Joy grabbed cups of coffee and stayed in the lobby.

"How did it go?" Shirley asked.

Anne looked Evelyn over from head to foot. "Are you okay? Did it go as planned?"

Evelyn felt like crying with happiness and relief. "It did go as planned. Seamus and Rafe heard Dr. Langer and Oscar admit that they took the coin and then used it to frame me for the crime. They also admitted that she paid him to get her into the museum. It was all her idea. They both have been arrested and should be coming through here soon. I gave a statement to the police, and Seamus is still in there talking to them. They told me I was free to go."

"That's wonderful," Joy said as she hugged Evelyn. "Well done. I'm so happy for you."

"Thank you for your support," Evelyn said to her friends. "I couldn't have done it without you."

"Oh, pshaw." Shirley laughed. "You're a brave and courageous lady."

"I don't feel brave," Evelyn said. "Just desperate."

"Is James still waiting for you?" Anne asked. "He's probably going wild with worry."

"He's in the car." Evelyn hugged Shirley and then Anne. "I should get out to him. Thanks, again. I'll see you all tomorrow."

"Bye!" The ladies echoed their goodbyes as Evelyn walked out to find James.

He jumped out of the car upon seeing her. His face was strained with worry, and his eyes sought hers for answers. “How did it go?”

The tears came then—the ones she’d been holding in all day. Through the unexpected arrival of the police, the search through her home, finding the coin, getting handcuffed and arrested, and then in making and executing the plans to get Dr. Langer and Oscar to confess, she had been close to tears. But now, as she fell into James’s embrace, the emotions overwhelmed her and she could barely catch her breath.

“Oh, Evelyn,” James said. “It’ll be okay. We’ll find another way. This isn’t the end.”

“No.” Evelyn shook her head, realizing that he was thinking the worst. She pulled back to look at him. “They confessed—they admitted to taking the coin and then trying to frame me. I’m free.”

The joy on his face was the most wonderful thing she’d ever seen in her life. He pulled her back into his arms, tighter this time. “Thank You, God,” he said on a whispered prayer. “Thank You for keeping Evelyn safe and for delivering her from this accusation.”

“Amen,” Evelyn echoed. “I just want to go home and eat and put on some comfortable clothes and relax.”

“Yes, ma’am.” James’s voice had lightened, and he almost did a jig as he opened Evelyn’s door and waited for her to get in.

They stopped for Chinese takeout on the way home, and Evelyn tried to call Shelby again, but she didn’t answer.

As they pulled into their driveway, Evelyn had never been happier to see her house. It was so dear and comforting.

James and Evelyn went inside and set the food on the kitchen counter.

"I'll go see if Shelby is back," Evelyn said.

She walked up the stairs and down the hall to Shelby's bedroom, saying a silent prayer for her safety and for their relationship, hoping that Shelby hadn't run away.

"Knock, knock," Evelyn said as she slowly opened the door.

Her niece was sitting on the floor of her room, folding her clothes. She looked up, and Evelyn could see that she had been crying. Her eyes and nose were puffy and red.

The two of them looked at each other for several moments before Evelyn stepped into the room and took a seat on the bed. She felt weary to her bones—and horrible for how she had turned on Shelby that morning.

"I tried calling you several times today," Evelyn said. "I even texted, but you didn't text back."

Shelby stood and went to the nightstand, where her phone was plugged into a charger. "I left it here when I went out today. I haven't looked at it since I got back."

Evelyn patted the spot next to her. "Come and sit with me, Shelby."

For a moment, Shelby stayed where she was, staring down at her phone. But then she set it on the bedside table and took a seat beside Evelyn.

"I'm sorry," Evelyn said. "I was upset and confused this morning. I should never have accused you—again."

Shelby just shrugged.

"I was wrong and scared. Though none of those things gave me the right to lash out at you."

"What's going to happen now? Will you go to jail?"

"I was in and out of jail already," Evelyn said. "But I won't be going back. I was able to prove to the police that two other people took the coin and tried to frame me. I've been cleared of all charges."

Joy lit up Shelby's eyes as she studied Evelyn. "So it's all done?"

"It's all done." Evelyn smiled. "The coin has been found, the culprits caught, and the museum is ready for the grand opening this weekend. I still have some last-minute things to deal with, but all the hard work is completed."

Shelby surprised Evelyn by reaching over and giving her a big hug. "I'm so happy you won't be going to jail."

"Me too." Evelyn squeezed her back.

Slowly, Shelby let her go. "My dad is coming for me on Sunday. He texted me late last night. I was going to tell you this morning, but everything was happening so quickly. He said my mom moved into her apartment, and she's ready for me. I'll pack everything up at home and fly out next Tuesday."

"A week from tomorrow?"

Shelby nodded.

"So, that means we only have six more days until your dad comes." Evelyn's heart felt heavy at the news. "I'm sorry that so much of your visit has been ruined by the coin theft."

A smile tilted Shelby's mouth. "It wasn't all bad. I had some fun being Queenie Bennett. You and Uncle James helped me get rid of Rodney, once and for all, and I had a really good time with you this past weekend." She put her hand on Evelyn's arm. "And I'm going to work really hard so I can come back next year and go to college in Charleston. You reminded me that the decisions my parents have made for me, up until this point, don't have to determine the rest of my life. I'll be in charge after next year, and it's my responsibility to make my life what I want it to be."

"Oh, Shelbs," Evelyn said as she pulled her back into an embrace. "You're turning into such an amazing young lady. I'm so proud of you."

"Thank you, Aunt Evelyn."

Evelyn wiped the tears that were falling down her cheeks again. "But no more crying. We still have a few days left to have a little fun. We brought home Chinese takeout. I hope you like it."

"I love Chinese food."

Evelyn rose and picked up Shelby's clothes from the floor and put them into the bureau.

"How does comfy clothes and another old movie sound to you?" Evelyn asked.

"As long as it can be *Singin' in the Rain*. I haven't seen that one since I was here last either."

"You got it." Evelyn started to hum as she put away Shelby's clothes.

It felt good to be happy again.

Chapter Twenty-One

THE DAY OF THE GRAND opening for the Mercy Hospital Museum was not quite what Evelyn had hoped or expected—at least, weather-wise. Instead of a bright and shining sky, low clouds hung over the Charleston peninsula, pouring rain down on the earth in a steady tempo. Out in the harbor, the precipitation and fog were so thick that Evelyn couldn't even see Fort Sumter from the hospital's windows. Everything was dreary and gloomy, and the temperatures had plummeted.

"Don't worry," Joy said as she helped set out the platters of cookies a local bakery had made for the special occasion. Earlier, she and Anne had put up a banquet-style table along one of the walls in the museum to serve the refreshments. "With this dismal weather, everyone will be looking for something to do, and they'll remember to come to the grand opening."

"I hope you're right," Evelyn said as she arranged a potted plant that had been sent from the South Carolina Historical Society as a grand opening gift. "Either that, or it'll prevent people from wanting to leave their snug houses."

"Let's be positive and hopeful." Shirley took a pink carnation corsage from its packaging and motioned for Evelyn to come over so she could pin it to the lapel of Evelyn's light gray blazer. "Even if no one but the governor comes, it'll be worth all the effort."

Evelyn stood patiently as Shirley attached the beautiful corsage. The flowers had arrived earlier that morning without a note, addressed to Evelyn. Somehow, they matched her gray and pink outfit perfectly. She suspected that James was responsible for the gift.

"How many people are you expecting?" Anne asked.

"It's hard to know. I was hoping that the article about the new museum in the *Charleston Times* would help bring in more people."

"If that article doesn't," Shirley said, throwing away the corsage packaging, "the one about Dr. Langer and Oscar Maverick's arrests might do the trick."

The front page of every newspaper in Charleston had covered the story. Thankfully, none of them had mentioned Evelyn's part in the whole ordeal but had said that the police department, in cooperation with the Mercy Hospital security staff, had uncovered the truth.

Evelyn and her friends worked to get the space ready as the rain continued to pour. James and Shelby would be coming soon, as would all the other guests.

"Someone's here to see you," Joy said as she nodded toward the museum door.

Mr. Lorenzo entered with a metal case in hand. He wasn't smiling, but he didn't look quite as unhappy as the last time Evelyn saw him. He approached her and gave her a curt nod.

"Hello, Mrs. Perry."

"It's nice to see you again, Mr. Lorenzo." She clasped her hands together and smiled. "What brings you here?"

"I had an emergency board meeting yesterday to discuss the coin." He lifted the metal case he was carrying. "Given all the information the police have supplied us with, we've decided to loan it to you, as agreed upon, after all."

Evelyn's mouth parted at the unexpected news. The display case and plaque were still intact, though she and Adam hadn't anticipated the return of the coin.

"I talked to Adam Chilton, and he said you still have the right tools available to get into the display case." Mr. Lorenzo looked around as he spoke. "I'd be happy to put it back myself. If"—he stared at Evelyn—"I can be guaranteed you've taken all the necessary precautions to avoid another theft."

"Yes," Evelyn said quickly. "We've installed more security cameras and have placed locks on the entrance to the tunnel."

"Good." He looked around again. "Can I get those tools?"

Evelyn showed him to the storage closet, which she unlocked, and helped him find what he needed to open the display case.

As he was working, Evelyn told her friends the good news but was quickly interrupted by another familiar face.

"Evelyn!" Jerica Dixon waved at Evelyn as she entered the museum. "I see the coin is back. That's good."

"Very good. I'm still trying to absorb the surprise." Evelyn smiled. "Your visit to Charleston must be coming to an end soon."

"Not until I talk to the governor. That's the whole reason I came, after all. I know he'll give it back to me once I explain everything properly."

Evelyn wasn't sure he would, but she glanced at Mr. Lorenzo as he set the coin inside the case. It was shiny and bright, reflecting the museum lighting perfectly. The truth was, there was little chance that Jerica would win her battle for it. A judge had deemed it a spoil of war, which meant it belonged to the United States of America. There was little the governor could do to change that fact.

Maybe what Jerica needed was a little truth. "Sometimes the hardest thing to do is let go of something we love. The coin is being cared for by the very best team of conservationists in the South. And, more than that, if it stays with the conservation center, thousands of people will get to see it and learn about George and Queenie's love story. People who might never have known who they were. As hard as it may be, it's right where it belongs, don't you think?"

"I just want people to know that we are part of its story," she said.

Evelyn nodded. She could appreciate that. "I would be happy to put your family name on the plaque. Then everyone will know that it's part of your heritage."

Jerica's eyes filled with joy. "You would do that?"

"Of course I would."

"That's all I really want—just to be recognized." Jerica smiled and then left Evelyn and went to Mr. Lorenzo. As he worked, she watched, asking questions about the coin that he was happy to answer.

"It occurred to me," Shirley said as she joined Evelyn, "that the coin represents more than just sunken dreams."

"Yeah?" Evelyn asked. "What else do you think it represents?"

"It represents hope. First, when it was given to a soldier, about to leave for war, it represented the hope that Queenie would see her lieutenant again. Then, when it saved George Dixon's life, it represented hope that it would continue to be a token of luck for him. Finally, when it was recovered off that submarine, it offered hope to everyone who has seen it since, that lost things can be found again."

Evelyn smiled. "It sure offers me a lot of hope. It's a reminder that God answers prayers and that good will ultimately prevail."

"I like that." Shirley grinned.

Anne and Joy finished putting out the treats and then joined them.

Joy pointed at the door, where half a dozen people were standing, among them, Adam and Stacia. "It looks like people are starting to arrive."

Evelyn glanced at her phone, which she was storing in her pocket in case of last-minute problems. "The governor should be here in about thirty minutes."

"Are you ready?" Anne asked.

Mr. Lorenzo was just finishing with the coin display, and Jerica was already wandering around the museum, looking over the exhibits.

Everything was in its proper place. There was nothing left for Evelyn to do but celebrate this wonderful accomplishment.

"I think we're ready." Evelyn saw James and Shelby walk up to the door as well. "Let's go open the doors and welcome our guests."

"Would you like to do the honors?" Joy asked.

"With pleasure." Evelyn walked to the double-glass doors and opened the one on the right and then the one on the left. She secured them in place and smiled at those who had already arrived. Among the gathering crowd were Earl, Garrison, and Seamus. People who had worked hard to make the museum a success—and she would tell all of them in the dedication speech she planned to give in an hour or so, after the governor arrived.

"Welcome," she said. "Come on in and see what wonderful history has shaped Mercy Hospital."

It didn't take long for the museum to fill up with friends, neighbors, and strangers, all of them eager to see the new exhibits. And as it did, Evelyn's heart began to swell with pride and joy. It had been a long road to this day, but seeing her dreams become a reality was worth all the effort.

Sunday came much too soon for Evelyn. Eric was scheduled to arrive for Shelby at three that afternoon, so Evelyn and James had taken her to church and then out to lunch. The rain had cleared overnight, and the sun shone bright and hot as they left the restaurant and walked along the seawall facing Charleston Harbor.

"I'll miss Queenie," Shelby said as she gave Evelyn a sly smile. "It was kind of fun to pretend to be someone else for a little while."

"Maybe you'd enjoy going into the history field and doing living history reenactment," James suggested as he cleaned his sunglasses before putting them back on.

"Oh," Shelby said, "I like that idea. Are there really jobs like that?"

"Absolutely." Evelyn nodded. "There are several historic sites right here in South Carolina that offer living history reenactments. But each state has places that hire historians for that purpose."

"I can think of several famous locations that offer world-class historical reenactment, like Colonial Williamsburg in Virginia and Old Sturbridge Village in Massachusetts. There are endless locations all over the United States—it all depends on what part of history you want to pursue."

"And," Evelyn said as she linked arms with her niece, "you won't have to hide your real identity."

Shelby grinned.

When they arrived at home, Shelby had just enough time to pack and get all of her things to the front door before her dad's expected arrival time.

Shelby, James, and Evelyn were in the kitchen when the doorbell rang.

"That'll be my dad," Shelby said as she let out a long sigh.

"You're always welcome to come back," Evelyn said as James went to answer the door. "And you can call or text me whenever you like, no matter the hour."

"Really?"

"Absolutely." Evelyn walked around the counter and gave Shelby a hug. "I love you."

"I love you too."

Eric entered the front hall and paused as he took in his daughter.

Shelby wore a pair of shorts with a nice blouse and a pair of flip-flops. Her hair was clean and tucked behind her ears, and she was only wearing a little bit of mascara. She looked fresh and bright as she met her dad's surprised gaze.

"Hi, Eric," Evelyn said.

"Hey." He still hadn't torn his eyes off Shelby. Finally, he said, "You look great, Shelbs."

She didn't smile for her dad—but she didn't put on an attitude either. She simply watched him.

"We just started brewing a pot of coffee," James said as he closed the door and then put his hand on Eric's shoulder. "Why don't you take a few minutes before heading back to Jacksonville."

"I kind of wanted to get on the road as soon as possible," Eric said, but then he smiled. "I guess we can stay for a few minutes. I have a feeling there's a lot to talk about."

Eric took a seat next to his daughter on one of the counter stools while James poured coffee and Evelyn took some lemon cookies out of the cabinet.

"How did everything go?" Eric finally asked.

Evelyn glanced at Shelby, who met her gaze. They shared a small smile. Eric knew quite a bit about what had happened after they discovered that Shelby and Rodney were behind the videos of Queenie. But Evelyn hadn't talked to him much this week. She didn't really want to get into the whole coin ordeal, so she simply said, "It was a little rocky at the beginning, but everything worked out in the end, didn't it, Shelby?"

"Yeah," she said with another smile. "It did."

Eric accepted his cup of coffee and took a sip. "I wasn't sure if I'd wait to tell Shelby this in private or not, but I think everyone deserves to know that Rodney was arrested and is facing criminal charges—and not just for the crimes we know about. He had a warrant out for a few other things." He looked at Shelby. "Rodney won't be bothering you again, baby."

Shelby bit her bottom lip and nodded.

Evelyn and James shared a glance, and Evelyn was certain that James was just as relieved as she was to hear this news.

"And," Eric added, "your mom told me that she broke up with her boyfriend. When you get to California, it'll just be the two of you."

For the first time since Shelby arrived, Evelyn saw real hope in her eyes. "Really?"

"Yep." He touched her arm. "I hope the two of you are able to work things out. Last time I talked to her, she sounded like she was realizing the mistakes she'd made and is ready to start trying."

Shelby put her hand on her dad's arm. "Does that mean you'll be getting back together?"

Eric's face fell, and he looked down at his coffee. "I don't think so, Shelbs. Right now, if the two of you can find reconciliation, I'll consider that enough."

Disappointment clouded Shelby's gaze, but she swallowed and took a deep breath.

"I'll be praying for you," Evelyn said to Shelby. "I hope your year in California is exactly what you and your mom need."

"Dad." Shelby pressed her lips together for a moment. "I want to come back to Charleston next year for college."

It took Eric a second, but he nodded. "I'd like that. Charleston is a great city. You'd love living here."

Shelby smiled at him and then lifted her gaze to Evelyn.

Evelyn winked at her, happy to hear her call Eric "Dad" again.

"I'm going to go make sure I didn't forget anything in my room," Shelby said as she got off her stool. "I'll be back, and then we can go."

"Okay, kiddo."

Shelby left the kitchen and bounded up the stairs.

Eric looked at James and then Evelyn. "Whatever you did to help Shelby, thank you, from the bottom of my heart. She looks and sounds like her old self again."

"It was our pleasure," Evelyn said as she reached across the counter and rubbed her brother's forearm. "We're here for both of you—you know that, right?"

"I do." He used his free hand to pat hers. "I appreciate all you've done for us. I'd like to give you something for keeping her."

"No need." James smiled. "Having Shelby here was a blessing to all of us, especially at a very difficult time. Both of you are always welcome—no strings attached."

"The same is true for me," Eric said. "I don't have much to offer, but whatever I have, it's yours if you're ever in need."

"Thank you, Eric." Evelyn walked around the counter and gave her brother a hug.

They visited for a few more minutes before Shelby was back, ready to go. Eric finished his cup of coffee and then they were at the front door.

Shelby gave James a hug and then Evelyn. "Thank you," she said, over and over again. "I love you both."

"Goodbye!" Evelyn called as the two of them walked out to Eric's car. "Call or text me when you can."

"I will." Shelby turned one last time and waved. "Bye!"

After they got into their car and pulled away, Evelyn and James walked back into the house and closed the front door.

It felt quieter than usual as they stood in the hallway, just smiling at each other.

"Thank you," Evelyn said to her husband.

"For what?" he asked as he pulled her into his arms.

"For loving me, for believing in me, and for always standing strong beside me."

"Our thirty-sixth year is going to be our best yet, Evie."

"You think so?"

"I know so." He tilted his head toward the kitchen. "How about we clean up the coffee and then go watch a good movie together?"

"I like that idea."

As James pulled away and walked toward the kitchen, Evelyn let out a contented sigh.

She was looking forward to all that the next year had in store for them—whatever that might be.

Dear Reader,

A few years ago, when my husband and I visited Charleston, we only had about a day and a half to see the city. One of my regrets was that we didn't visit the Warren Lasch Conservation Center to see the *H.L. Hunley* on display. I had heard about it but didn't realize the significance of the submarine until after we returned home. Once I learned its history, I knew I wanted to incorporate it into one of the stories I wrote for the Sweet Carolina Mysteries series. The submarine's use in the Civil War, and its subsequent discovery in Charleston Harbor over a hundred and thirty years later, is amazing. But when you add the history of Lieutenant George Dixon, the twenty-dollar gold coin that saved his life, and his love story with Queenie Bennett, it reminds me that fact is often stranger than fiction.

I hope you felt like you visited Charleston while reading *Sunken Hopes*. It's so much fun to set a story in the historic district and return there in my imagination. I can't wait to get back in person someday soon.

Enjoy!

Signed,
Gabrielle Meyer

About the Author

Gabrielle Meyer lives on the banks of the upper Mississippi River in central Minnesota with her husband and four children. As an employee of the Minnesota Historical Society, she fell in love with history and enjoys writing historical, contemporary, and cozy mystery novels inspired by the past. When Gabrielle is not writing, you might find her homeschooling her children, cheering them on at sporting and theatrical events, or hosting a gathering at her home with family and friends. You can learn more by visiting her at GabrielleMeyer.com.

The Story Behind the Story

On February 17, 1864, the *H.L. Hunley* became the first submarine to sink a warship in combat history. It sank the Union warship, USS *Housatonic,* in Charleston Harbor, taking the lives of five Union soldiers, and then mysteriously disappeared. For over a hundred years, no one knew what had happened to the submarine, but in 1995 it was discovered one hundred yards away from where the *Housatonic* went down, in just twenty-seven feet of water. The *Hunley* was buried under several feet of silt, concealing and protecting it for a future generation to discover.

It took almost five years to raise enough money to recover the submarine, but in August of 2000, it was finally pulled from the bottom of the harbor. There were so many questions surrounding the sunken vessel, many of which were answered, though some remain to this day. It's still unclear why the submarine didn't resurface. The crew of eight Confederate soldiers was found, each in his position within the submarine, and there was no apparent cause of death. Some think that the shock from detonating the missile that took down the *Housatonic* stunned the *Hunley,* rendering the crew unconscious, at which point, the submarine took on water and drowned the men.

One of the things that stands out to me the most is the bravery of the soldiers on board the *Hunley.* Before the fateful night it was lost, it had already taken the lives of thirteen other men, including the inventor and namesake, Horace Lawson Hunley, in two separate test runs. I can't imagine the courage, and the pure dedication to their cause, that propelled those men into the submarine in 1864.

After the submarine was painstakingly preserved and the remains of the men were examined by forensic anthropologists, the men were laid to rest in Magnolia Cemetery in Charleston. Tens of thousands of people came out for the ceremony, including six thousand reenactors and four thousand citizens in period clothing.

But one of the most amazing discoveries was that of the coin, found near the remains of Lieutenant George Dixon, the captain of the vessel. For over a hundred years, the Dixon family had shared the legend of the coin, given to George from his sweetheart, Queenie Bennett, which saved his life at the Battle of Shiloh. It was just a legend until the coin was actually found! It can still be viewed at the Warren Lasch Conservation Center, along with the rest of the submarine, in Charleston.

Good for What Ails You

Cold-Busting Chicken Noodle Soup with Ginger

Ingredients:

- 1 ½ tablespoons olive oil
- 3 large chicken breasts
- 1 large onion, diced
- 3 cloves garlic, crushed
- 13 cups water
- 2 cups white wine
- ¾ cup fresh lemon juice
- 1 (4 inch) piece fresh ginger, peeled and thinly sliced
- 7 whole black peppercorns
- 4 cubes chicken bouillon
- 3 bay leaves
- 1 tablespoon white sugar
- ¾ cup peeled and sliced carrots
- 2 stalks celery, diced
- 1 kohlrabi bulb, peeled and diced
- 2 ½ tablespoons fresh rosemary
- 2 tablespoons fresh thyme
- 1 (8 ounce) package egg noodles
- 1 large clove garlic, minced
- 1 tablespoon grated ginger
- 1 teaspoon salt, or to taste
- ½ cup chopped fresh parsley

Directions:

Step 1: Heat olive oil in large pot over medium heat. Add chicken, onion, and crushed garlic cloves; cook in hot oil until chicken breast is browned and onions start to turn translucent, about 5 minutes. Pour water, white wine, and lemon juice over the chicken mixture; stir sliced ginger, peppercorns, chicken bouillon, bay leaves, and white sugar into the liquid. Bring to simmer, reduce heat to medium-low, and cook for 45 minutes.

Step 2: Remove and discard crushed garlic cloves. Remove chicken breasts from soup to cutting board; chop into bite-sized pieces.

Step 3: Add carrots, celery, kohlrabi, rosemary, and thyme to soup. Reduce heat to low until the vegetables begin to soften, about 20 minutes.

Step 4: Bring soup to boil. Return chopped chicken to soup along with egg noodles, minced garlic, and grated ginger; remove pot from heat and let sit until noodles have softened, about 10 minutes. Season with salt. Garnish with parsley.

Read on for a sneak peek of another exciting book in the Sweet Carolina Mysteries series!

Hair Today, Gone Tomorrow

BY LESLIE GOULD

JOY ATKINS SPUN THE GREETING card display stand around, noting the collection of Father's Day cards with a lump in her throat. The holiday was just over a week away.

Several customers who had been shopping for a Get Well card in the last week chose a Father's Day card—or two—as well. Several hospital staff had purchased them too, grateful for the convenience. Joy suspected she'd sell even more cards during the week ahead.

Father's Day was still a hard time for Joy, two years after her husband, Wilson, had passed. Thankfully her daughter, Sabrina, had her own husband to celebrate, with the help of their two daughters. But Joy knew it was a hard day for all of them too. Wilson had been a wonderful father and grandfather, not to mention a fantastic husband.

She'd always hosted a barbecue back at their home in Texas, starting when Sabrina was six months old. Back then, Joy's father had been one of the honored guests. Friends and neighbors attended too. Wilson manned the grill, cooking ribs and brats. After she was grown, Sabrina and her family would travel from Charleston to attend. It had been one of Joy's favorite days of the year.

She stepped away from the cards and resumed dusting the collection of vases. Life changed. Nothing remained the same. Here she was in Charleston now, blessed to be close to Sabrina and her family.

Still, she missed Wilson every single day. And, honestly, every time someone bought a Father's Day card she felt a pang of grief. She was going to change that. From now on, she'd pray for that family—and other families too—that they'd be blessed as they celebrated.

A commotion in the lobby caught Joy's attention, and she stepped to the window, her duster still in hand. Sassie Crane, who wore a black blouse, a leopard print pencil skirt, and strappy sandals, was hurrying toward the lobby exit with a man following behind her. Joy stepped to the doorway of the gift shop. Sassie caught sight of her and veered for the door, dodging in front of an older couple and slipping inside the shop as the man kept going.

Joy stayed in the doorway for a minute, but the man didn't return. He had thick gray hair, was rather tall and lean, and wore a goatee. Joy didn't recognize him.

Joy stepped back into the shop but didn't see Sassie at first. Finally she spotted her examining a blown glass vase, her long dark bangs from her asymmetrical haircut hanging over one eye.

"What was that all about?" Joy asked.

Sassie raised her head, flipped her bangs aside, and met Joy's gaze. "I'm not sure." Sassie laughed a little. "A case of mistaken identity, I'm sure." She held up the seafoam-colored vase. "This is perfect for the addition to my spa—I'm going to have a big reopening in two weeks. The palette is sea cottage chic. Pastels and neutrals. I'll take it."

Not only was *chic* a good adjective for Sassie's décor in her expanded spa, but it was for Sassie too. Joy guessed, by the age of Sassie's daughter, that Sassie was in her midfifties, but she could easily pass for forty.

As Joy rang up the vase, she debated whether to ask about Sassie's waiting list. Joy had been on it for over a month, hoping to have Sassie, who was the premier stylist in Charleston, cut her hair.

Finally, as she ran Sassie's card, she said, "Any chance you have an opening on your wait list?"

"That's right, you are on *that* list," Sassie said. "As a matter of fact, I had a cancellation this morning and haven't had a chance to fill it. If you'd like, it's yours."

"What time?" Joy wrapped the vase in tissue paper.

"Three thirty today."

"Perfect," Joy said. "I'll be there." She had nothing else planned for her late Friday afternoon.

Sassie's daughter, Ashley, was friends with Sabrina. Joy had met Ashley when she first moved to Charleston, and then she had met Sassie at a garden party a couple of months ago.

Of course Joy had known of Sassie before then. She owned and operated Sassie's Salon and Spa, which was located kitty-corner from the hospital in the historic Crane Building. Joy sometimes got pedicures there with her friend Shirley and Shirley's mother, Regina, but she hadn't been able to get an appointment for a haircut.

Joy placed the vase in a bag.

"Thank you." Sassie gave Joy another smile as she took the purchase. "See you at three."

Perplexed, Joy said, "Three thirty? That's what you just said."

"Right." Sassie smiled again. "Three thirty. See you then."

Joy switched the sign to Closed at three.

As she stepped out the door, closed it, and then began to lock it, Evelyn Perry, the director of the hospital's records department called out, "Hello, Joy! Where are you off to this early?" Evelyn wore her silver hair in a bun on her head with a pencil tucked in it.

Joy often stuck around until three thirty or four, especially on a Friday, to tidy up for the weekend. Joy waved at her friend. "I finally got a hair appointment with Sassie."

Evelyn smiled. "I was just thinking about her."

"Any reason why?"

"I could swear I saw her cousin in the lobby this morning."

Joy tilted her head. "Which was unexpected, I'm guessing?"

Evelyn nodded. "On the other hand, perhaps it wasn't him at all. I haven't seen him in thirty years, which doesn't mean he hasn't been around, but the man is how I imagine her cousin would look now."

"Gray hair and a goatee?"

Evelyn tilted her head. "How did you know?"

"I saw a man who looked like that following Sassie through the lobby this morning, right before she came into the shop."

Evelyn shrugged. "I'm probably imagining things." She gave Joy a wave. "Have fun getting your haircut."

"Thanks! Have a wonderful weekend."

"You too." Evelyn smiled and continued on toward the records department.

As Joy stepped out of the main entrance of the hospital, she took her cell phone from her purse and pressed Sabrina's number.

The call went straight to voice mail. Joy said hello and then, "Guess what? I'm on my way to Sassie's for a haircut. Talk to you soon!"

Joy held her phone in her hand as she waited for the crosswalk signal to change. Once it did, as she crossed the street, her phone buzzed. A text from Sabrina. GREAT! HAVE FUN! MAYBE I'LL SEE YOU LATER—I'M GOING TO HAVE DINNER WITH ASHLEY WHILE ROB TAKES THE GIRLS TO PLAY TENNIS. ELOISE KEEPS SAYING SHE WANTS TO LEARN. IT'S COOL ENOUGH THAT I THINK I'LL RIDE MY BIKE.

Joy "loved" the text and then slipped her phone back into her purse. Rob had given Sabrina a bicycle for Mother's Day, and she'd been riding whenever she could, with the girls and by herself, often with their dog Mopsy on a leash and running along beside her in their neighborhood. But sometimes she went on a long solo bike ride, just for fun.

Ahead of her was the entrance to Sassie's Salon and Spa. The two-story Crane Building took up a small, odd-sized block. The second floor was all apartments. The front side, which faced the bay, was a line of shops, including Sassie's. The back side was a warehouse. Sassie was remodeling half the space to expand her spa. Joy guessed, with the demand for retail space in the downtown area, that the rest of the warehouse would soon be repurposed too and rented out. Sassie had an amazing resource in the building, along with an admirable business that she'd built since she was a young woman.

Joy continued on, pushing through the front door. The interior of the shop was decorated in what seemed to already be a sea cottage chic theme. The walls were a seafoam green while the accents were tan, teal, and rose. A sea salt candle burned on the counter, filling the shop with the scent of the sun on warm waves.

Ashley stood at the counter. She had her mother's dark hair, although she wore it long and straight. "Joy," she said. "How nice to see you. What can I do for you?"

"I have a three thirty appointment with your mom."

Ashley glanced down at the appointment book in front of her.

"She told me she had a cancellation. I was on the wait list."

"Oh. I don't remember Hannah ever canceling before." Ashley glanced up and smiled. "It's your lucky day."

Joy smiled back. "I agree."

"Take a seat," Ashley said. "She'll be ready in a few minutes."

"I'm early," Joy said.

Ashley smiled. "You'll have time for a cup of tea. Or a glass of water."

"I'll take the water."

Ashley stepped to a beverage bar off to the side and filled a glass, pouring from a pitcher of ice water and sliced limes. Joy took the glass and settled in a pale pink leather chair next to a tabletop water fountain and leaned her head against the back of the chair. She could hear the buzz of a power tool. She turned toward the noise, coming from the inner part of the building.

"We're turning the first floor of the warehouse into our expanded spa," Ashley said.

"That's right," Joy said. "Your mother mentioned that this morning."

"We'll have a grand reopening in two weeks."

"That sounds lovely."

After a moment of silence, Ashley said, "I'm having dinner with Sabrina tonight."

"That's what she told me," Joy said. "It's a rare night off for her."

"Seriously," Ashley said. "I've been wanting to get together with her forever."

"She's longed for that too."

Ashley's husband, Barry, had died six months before during a freak sailing accident. Sabrina, along with her best friend from college, Amanda, had been there for Ashley as much as they could after the tragedy.

"Is Amanda joining you?"

Ashley shook her head. "She's working a long shift today." Amanda was a doctor at Mercy.

A couple of minutes later, Sassie appeared in the doorway and said, "Come on back, Joy" just as a tall woman with beautiful auburn hair came striding through the front door.

"Hannah," Ashley said and then spun toward her mother.

"Hannah," Sassie echoed. "You canceled your appointment."

The woman shrugged. "I changed my mind."

A few minutes later, Joy sat in one salon chair in Sassie's studio while Hannah sat next to her. The other of the four chairs were filled with the clients of two additional stylists. Everyone but Joy was talking. She sat silently, listening.

Sassie stood behind Hannah's chair. "I'll get Joy started first with her color and then get started on yours."

Hannah wrinkled her nose.

Sassie patted the woman on the shoulder. "You can't cancel your appointment and expect me not to fill it."

"But it's been my appointment for the last thirty years."

"Thirty-seven," Sassie retorted. "No, thirty-eight."

Hannah sighed. "Who's counting?"

Both Sassie and Hannah looked amazing. Joy couldn't believe they were in their midfifties.

Hannah lowered her voice. "Parker was acting strange this morning. That's why I canceled. I was hoping to get him a doctor's appointment."

"How is he this afternoon?"

"Better."

"Maybe it's his new medication."

"Maybe…" Hannah took a sip from the metal bottle she held in her hand. "I want to talk with the doctor about that. We have an appointment for Wednesday."

Sassie patted Hannah's shoulder again, this time gently. "Did you bring a book?"

Hannah smiled and reached in her big handbag that was still in her lap. "I did."

"Good girl," Sassie said. "I'll be with you in no time."

"You could go ahead and do Hannah's color first," Joy said, feeling as if she'd stolen Hannah's appointment.

Hannah shook her head. "No. Sassie's right. I canceled."

"But I'm not in a hurry," Joy said. "I'm happy to wait."

Hannah pursed her lips. "I do need to pick up Lindsay at five thirty."

"Are you sure, Joy?" Sassie asked.

"Positive." Joy reached for her bag and then pulled *Growing Peonies in the South* from it. "I brought a book too."

"Bless your heart." Sassie patted Joy's shoulder and turned her attention toward Hannah, although she continued speaking to Joy. "I've been doing Hannah's hair since I graduated from beauty school." Sassie paused a moment. "Actually since high school. She used to let me experiment on her. God bless her soul for all of eternity for trusting me the way she did."

Hannah grinned. "Remember the Farrah Fawcett hairdo you gave me? Every single hair was layered. And dyed blond."

Sassie laughed. "Sophomore year. Parker took one look at you and asked you to the prom, even though he was a senior."

"And I turned him down to go with Ernest." There was a long, awkward pause and then Hannah said, "A week later you dyed my hair auburn." Hannah touched the ends of her hair as Sassie mixed the hair dye.

"And Parker loved that too," Sassie said.

"Ha." Hannah shook her head. "Not as much as I have. We really were the Dream Team."

Sassie laughed. "Never forget that we started out as the Dare to Dream Team back in middle school."

"That was when it was just you and me, before we let the boys join. We were so desperate to make something ourselves."

"And we have." Sassie met her friend's eyes in the mirror.

Hannah smiled in agreement.

Joy opened her book and began reading, half listening to Sassie and Hannah's conversation. Lindsay was Hannah and Parker's daughter. It sounded as if she was in high school. No mention of other children was made.

"Do you remember Lindsay's nanny—Rochelle?"

Sassie murmured, "Yes, of course."

"She moved back to town. She has a baby of her own and asked Lindsay to babysit."

"How sweet."

"Except Lindsay has absolutely no time to babysit—" Hannah paused. "Nor the need. I was surprised Rochelle would even ask."

Joy glanced up from her book and snuck a quick look at Sassie. She seemed to be concentrating intensely on Hannah's hair until she literally bit her lip. Perhaps she was simply concentrating on not responding.

Positioning her book closer to her face, Joy reread the first paragraph and then kept reading. The more she read—that peonies could do well in the South, including South Carolina, but needed well-drained soil and lots of space—the less she was aware of the conversation going on next to her.

When Sassie stepped behind her, Joy was surprised she was done with applying the color to Hannah's hair already. Joy glanced toward her left. Hannah sat with her head slathered in dye, now reading her own book.

Sassie lifted a section of Joy's hair. "What do you have in mind?"

"The same color plus a good trim but with more texture."

"How about a shade lighter on the color? I think that will work with your skin tone, plus with summer starting it will give you a lift."

Joy hesitated.

"Believe me." Hannah looked up from her book. "Trust Sassie when it comes to your hair. And pretty much everything else too."

"Yes, trust me with your hair, but I don't know about *everything* else." Sassie slipped on a new pair of gloves. "I'm sure Joy has *everything* else figured out by now."

Joy smiled. "I'm sure no one has *everything* figured out, no matter how"—she cleared her throat and slowly said—"mature..."

Sassie laughed. "I wasn't implying that. You seem calm and collected is what I was getting at. Unlike some of us."

Joy couldn't imagine what Sassie was talking about. In every interaction she'd had with Sassie, she'd seemed more than calm and collected. She was a dignified woman who carried herself with confidence and grace and presented herself with a signature style. Even when being pursued through the lobby of the hospital that morning.

Instead of risking saying the wrong thing, Joy simply said, "A shade lighter sounds like fun." She watched in the mirror as Sassie mixed her color and then began applying it.

One of the stylists at the end of the row of chairs finished with her client and said, "They're ready for you in the spa."

"Great." The woman wiggled her toes. "I'm definitely ready for my pedicure."

The stylist walked the woman through the far door and then returned. "See you tomorrow," she said to Sassie.

"See you then." Sassie glanced up from Joy's hair. "Thank you for your good work."

After the stylist exited to the lobby, Joy could hear her speaking with Ashley. In a low voice, Sassie said to Joy, "Your Sabrina has been such a good friend to my Ashley. She's really helped her through the last few months."

Empathy flooded through Joy. "I can't imagine going through everything Ashley has at such a young age."

"I know," Sassie said. "But still, you've been there. You know what Ashley's faced since Barry's passing, which is probably part of the reason Sabrina has been so understanding."

Joy hadn't thought of that connection, but it made sense. Sabrina had been a big support, even in her own grief, when Wilson passed away.

A thud startled Joy. Hannah's book had hit the floor. Sassie put the dye on the counter and bent to pick up the book. As she stood, she asked, "Hannah, are you all right?"

Hannah's head jerked. "I must have dozed off." She took the book from Sassie and then reached for her metal water bottle, which she'd placed on the counter. She took a drink and then replaced it, returning to her reading.

Sassie resumed spreading the dye on Joy's hair.

"How long have you had your salon?" Joy asked.

"I opened it up the day after I passed my state boards. I was nineteen years old."

"That's amazing."

"I didn't do it on my own," Sassie said. "My grandfather owned the building and gave me a big break on my lease. And a beautician who owned a salon in town gave me a deal on her equipment because she was retiring. I've had my challenges over the years, but for the most part, it's been a great run."

"No plans to retire?"

"Absolutely not," Sassie said. "Now that Ashley is working with me, I'm ready to go another twenty years at least."

Joy nodded. Sabrina had mentioned that Ashley was working with Sassie.

"With the upcoming expansion, I figure the best is yet to come," Sassie said. She finished spreading the dye over Joy's short hair. As Sassie turned toward the sink, another thud, this time louder, startled Joy and she jumped.

Hannah's metal bottle had hit the floor, followed by Hannah sliding out of the chair, her book falling out of her hand and smacking the tile too. Followed by the back of Hannah's head.

A Note from the Editors

We hope you enjoyed another exciting volume in the Sweet Carolina Mysteries series, published by Guideposts. For over seventy-five years, Guideposts, a nonprofit organization, has been driven by a vision of a world filled with hope. We aspire to be the voice of a trusted friend, a friend who makes you feel more hopeful and connected.

By making a purchase from Guideposts, you join our community in touching millions of lives, inspiring them to believe that all things are possible through faith, hope, and prayer. Your continued support allows us to provide uplifting resources to those in need. Whether through our online communities, websites, apps, or publications, we strive to inspire our audiences, bring them together, and comfort, uplift, entertain, and guide them.

To learn more, please go to guideposts.org.

A Note from the Author

[illegible]